One-Pan Vegan

The Simple Sheet Pan Solution for Fast,
Flavorful Plant-Based Cooking

Lucy Hosier, Creator of What Luce Eats

PAGE STREET
PUBLISHING CO.

PAGE STREET
PUBLISHING CO.

To my husband-to-be, Tom, for being chief taste tester, washer upper and my biggest cheerleader. Thank you for making me believe in myself.

Contents

Introduction

Four years ago, I was sitting behind a desk, working a mundane full-time insurance job in London. If I had predicted my future, I would not have imagined writing a cookbook (especially a vegan one) and moving 250 miles to the opposite side of the country.

It's thanks to my digestive troubles that I am where I am today, which might sound a bit peculiar. After experiencing digestive issues for a couple of years as a late teen and with my mum having celiac disease, I underwent various medical tests to get to the root cause of my problems. All tests came back with no issues, and as a final resort, my doctor advised me to try eliminating meat and dairy from my diet to see if that would help. So after a very indulgent holiday in January 2018 and my digestion being at its worst, I ditched all animal products and adopted a plant-based diet overnight. I've not had so much as a stomachache since!

In changing my diet, I immediately realized I needed to learn to cook or I was going to end up getting very bored with what I was eating. That process made me fall in love with experimenting in the kitchen. It became my favorite way to relax, and I'd spend my weekends following recipes and creating my own. I started to upload pictures of what I made and post them to my personal social media accounts. Within six months or so, I'd bought a camera, and my self-taught photography journey sat side-by-side with my passion to prove to others that eating plant-based foods doesn't have to be bland or boring.

Much to my amazement, my social media following started to grow, and within a year I was approached by my first client (Dr. Hazel Wallace from @thefoodmedic) to develop and photograph recipes for her audience. Fast forward ten months to October 2019, and I was able to quit my office job thanks to the opportunities that came my way.

I now live 250 miles north of London, eat and photograph food for a living. And when I'm not doing that, I'm exploring our beautiful surroundings in the countryside with my partner, Tom, and our miniature dachshunds, Banger and Beans. I'm forever grateful for how my life has turned out and hope that in twenty years I'm still jazzing up vegetables into gorgeous recipes in my kitchen and receiving the best feedback from the people that make my recipes.

Why write a cookbook?

Every recipe developer's dream is to write a cookbook, so when I was approached by Page Street and had the initial conversations with them, I knew straight away I had to say yes, pinching myself. My dream was coming true.

Often when I interact with my audiences on my blog or socials, I ask them what types of recipes they want. Nine times out of ten the answer is, "recipes that are easy and involve minimal fuss." So, that is what this cookbook is going to bring you. Most of the recipes involve tossing ingredients onto a sheet pan and into the oven to be transformed into a tasty dish in no time at all.

I want to not only prove it's simple to eat a diverse range of plant-based foods, but also to teach readers how to season and marinate said foods to make their taste buds sing with joy. There are no complicated ingredients involved, but hopefully some foods you may not have tried before. I don't believe in dieting and live on the principle of balance. I love fueling my body with nourishing foods, and I love the way they make me feel, but also enjoy an indulgent bake or two on the side. Life is way too short!

This book is not only targeted at vegans, but also those who just want to eat a few more veggies or do a bit more for the environment and/or animal welfare. I do not preach or pressure people into following a plant-based diet, but instead get a huge amount of joy knowing I may have added even one new plant-based recipe to somebody's recipe bank.

I really hope that you enjoy making and eating these recipes as much as I do, and that this book gets covered in dirty fingerprints from you making what's inside. I'd love for this book to get pride of place on your shelves.

US to UK Glossary of Terms

All-purpose flour — plain flour	Lima beans — butter beans
Broccolini — tenderstem broccoli	Oatmeal — porridge oats
Canned corn — canned sweetcorn	Scallions — spring onions
Cilantro — coriander	Super fine sugar — caster sugar
Confectioners' sugar — icing sugar	Vegan ground beef — vegan mince
Eggplant — aubergine	Zucchini — courgette

No-Fuss Breakfasts in 30 Minutes

Whether you're prepping breakfasts on a Sunday for a busy week ahead, or you've got several hungry mouths to feed in the morning, these one-sheet breakfast recipes are for you. This chapter includes both sweet and savory recipes you can choose depending on what you fancy. Plus, who wants to do tons of washing up first thing in the morning? Nope, me neither. Most of these recipes only require a sheet pan or tray and a bowl, so you can enjoy the first meal of your day alongside a strong brew with minimal cleanup afterward.

The scones (pages 22 and 25) are best eaten fresh (you deserve a medal if you can make them last a few days without devouring them anyway), but all the other recipes will stay fresh in an airtight container either in or out of the fridge for up to a week. So, you can enjoy the recipe again and again and again. For slower weekend mornings, my favorite is the Breakfast Tempeh Hash with Cashew "Cheese" (page 10). And for weekday mornings when a quick breakfast is needed, I love prepping the Berry Sheet Pancakes (page 13) the night before to be able to set my alarm that little bit later.

Breakfast Tempeh Hash with Cashew "Cheese"

If you haven't tried cashew cheese before, you've seriously been missing out. This dish is perfect for those fancying a savory breakfast or brunch, and the crispy potatoes paired with tempeh chunks that are bursting with flavor will be loved by all. You prepare the "cheese" while the rest is roasting away on the sheet pan. So although there are a few components to this dish, it won't take long to prepare at all.

Yield: 4 servings

1 cup (140 g) cashews

3⅓ cups (450 g) diced sweet potatoes, skin on

4 cups (560 g) diced white potatoes, skin on

½ white onion, diced

3 tbsp (45 ml) extra virgin olive oil, divided

1⅓ cups (200 g) diced tempeh

2 tbsp (30 ml) soy sauce

1 tsp garlic granules, divided

½ tsp cayenne pepper

½ tsp onion powder

1 red pepper, diced

½ cup (120 ml) oat milk or other dairy-free alternative

1 tbsp (10 g) nutritional yeast

2 cups (130 g) kale, stalks removed, chopped

3 scallions, sliced

1 tbsp (3 g) fresh chives, chopped

Pinch of chili flakes, optional

Preheat the oven to 350°F (180°C or gas mark 4). To a heatproof bowl, add the cashews and cover with boiling water and set aside.

Place the sweet and white potatoes along with the onion on a large sheet pan. Drizzle with 2 tablespoons (30 ml) of the olive oil and using a spoon or your hands, ensure the potatoes are covered evenly in the oil. Place the potatoes in the oven to roast for 15 minutes.

Meanwhile, place the diced tempeh into a bowl, then add the remaining tablespoon (15 ml) of olive oil plus the soy sauce, ½ teaspoon of the garlic granules, cayenne pepper and onion powder. Mix to combine.

Carefully remove the pan from the oven and add the tempeh and diced pepper, then place it back into the oven for another 15 minutes.

While the pan is in the oven, prepare the cashew cheese. Drain the cashews and place them in a high-speed blender along with the oat milk, nutritional yeast and remaining ½ teaspoon of garlic granules. Blend until smooth and creamy.

When the pan in the oven has 5 minutes remaining, spread the kale on top and place it back into the oven.

Serve the breakfast hash with the cashew "cheese," sliced scallions, chopped chives and chili flakes, if desired.

Berry Sheet Pancakes

Sheet pancakes are a game changer. I hate all the flipping involved when cooking on the stove, plus there's always a high chance of burning them. But not here! Feel free to use whatever berries you fancy, or you could add some chocolate chips if you like. I love prepping these on a Sunday and reheating during the week for breakfast. Pancakes all day, every day!

Yield: 4 servings

2½ cups (600 ml) dairy-free milk

2 tbsp (30 ml) maple syrup

1 tbsp (15 ml) vanilla extract

4⅓ cups (540 g) all-purpose flour

1 tbsp (15 g) baking powder

2 tbsp (15 g) ground flaxseed

½ cup (125 g) frozen raspberries, divided, plus more for serving

½ cup (100 g) frozen blueberries, divided, plus more for serving

Dairy-free yogurt

Preheat the oven to 350°F (180°C or gas mark 4) and place a piece of parchment paper on a half sheet pan (13 x 18 inches [33 x 45 cm]). In a large bowl, combine the milk, maple syrup and vanilla extract. Add the flour, baking powder and ground flaxseed, and mix until combined.

Fold half of the frozen raspberries and blueberries into the batter, then pour the mixture onto the sheet pan. Ensure it has reached all the corners and is evenly spread before topping with the remaining frozen berries.

Bake for 20 to 25 minutes, or until golden brown and a toothpick inserted in the pancake comes out clean. Allow the pancake to cool slightly before removing from the pan and slicing. Serve with your favorite yogurt and any extra berries.

Miso, Vanilla and Cinnamon Sheet Pan French Toast

Using miso paste in sweet dishes is delicious. The umami flavor pairs with the vanilla and cinnamon so well, and French toast is a great way to use up bread that's not so fresh. Using a sheet pan gives you much more space than a pan on the stove so you can cook all the slices at once, rather than in batches.

Yield: 2 servings

2 tbsp (30 g) melted dairy-free butter

1 tbsp (15 ml) maple syrup, plus more to drizzle

½ cup (120 ml) dairy-free milk

1 tsp miso paste

1 tbsp (15 ml) vanilla extract

1½ tbsp (11 g) ground flaxseed

½ tsp ground cinnamon

4 slices day-old sourdough bread

½ cup (70 g) sliced fresh strawberries

1 tbsp (8 g) coconut flakes

Preheat the grill or broil function on your oven to 480°F (250°C) and place a piece of parchment paper on a sheet pan.

In a shallow dish, combine the melted butter, maple syrup, milk, miso paste, vanilla extract, ground flaxseed and ground cinnamon.

Place the slices of bread into the mixture for a few seconds on each side, ensuring the whole slice is covered with the batter. Place the soaked slices onto the lined sheet pan and then place the pan in the oven under the broiler or grill.

Grill for 10 to 12 minutes on each side. Serve with the strawberries, coconut flakes and an extra drizzle of maple syrup.

Scrambled Tofu Breakfast Sheet

This is one of my all-time favorite breakfasts. I always make this for my non-vegan friends and family to show them how much yummier it is than eggs. Spreading the crumbled tofu mixture out thinly on the sheet pan means it only takes 20 minutes to transform this dish into one you will choose over scrambled eggs every time. Feel free to serve alongside something other than toasted sourdough, but in my opinion serving on top of toasted buttery sourdough with a drizzle of balsamic glaze is pure perfection. You can use normal firm tofu in this recipe, but I recommended using smoked tofu as it adds depth to the flavor.

Yield: 4 servings

1 tbsp (15 ml) extra virgin olive oil

2 tbsp (6 g) fresh chives, finely chopped

⅓ cup (80 ml) oat milk

2 tbsp (30 ml) soy sauce

¼ tsp smoked paprika

2 tbsp (10 g) nutritional yeast

1 clove garlic, crushed

½ tsp ground turmeric

3 scallions, sliced

Salt and pepper to taste

2 (8-oz [227-g]) blocks smoked tofu

For Serving

Toasted sourdough bread, buttered

Fresh sliced tomatoes

Balsamic glaze, optional

Preheat the oven to 350°F (180°C or gas mark 4).

In a large bowl, combine all the ingredients except the tofu. Crumble the tofu into the bowl and combine thoroughly until all the tofu is covered in the mixture.

Scatter the tofu onto a sheet pan and place it into the oven. Bake the tofu for 10 minutes, then carefully remove the pan and give the tofu a stir before placing it back into the oven for an additional 10 minutes.

Serve the scrambled tofu on top of the buttered toasted sourdough with some slices of fresh tomatoes. Drizzle with balsamic glaze, if you wish.

Mexican Sheet Pancakes with Guacamole

With a base similar to my Berry Sheet Pancakes (page 13), this recipe has a savory Mexican twist. If you're looking for something a little different, this recipe is the one for you. Sweet corn is such an underrated veggie in my opinion, and the crushed tortilla chips add a fabulous crunch.

Yield: 4 servings

4⅓ cups (540 g) all-purpose flour

1 tbsp (15 g) baking powder

1 tsp paprika

2 tsp (6 g) garlic powder

1 tsp chili flakes

4 scallions, sliced

3 tbsp (9 g) fresh chives, chopped

¾ tsp salt

2½ cups (600 ml) dairy-free milk

¾ cup (190 g) canned corn, drained

2 large avocados

1 red chili, finely diced

2 tbsp (30 ml) fresh lime juice

1¾ cups (250 g) cherry tomatoes, quartered

½ red onion, diced

1 tbsp (1 g) fresh cilantro, chopped

1 tbsp (15 ml) extra virgin olive oil

1 cup (25 g) crushed salted tortilla chips

Preheat the oven to 350°F (180°C or gas mark 4) and place a piece of parchment paper on a half sheet pan (13 x 18 inch [33 x 45 cm]). In a large bowl, combine the flour, baking powder, paprika, garlic powder, chili flakes, scallions, chives and salt.

Add the milk, combine until smooth and then fold in the corn. Transfer the mixture to the sheet pan and spread into the corners. Bake in the oven for 20 to 25 minutes, or until golden brown or a toothpick inserted into the pancake comes out clean.

Meanwhile, mash the avocados in a bowl and stir in the diced chili and lime juice. In a separate bowl, combine the cherry tomatoes, diced onion and cilantro.

When the pancakes are cooked, remove them from the oven and brush them with the olive oil, allowing it to sink into the pancakes. Allow the pancake to cool for 5 minutes before slicing and stacking on a plate. Top with the avocado, cherry tomato mixture and crushed tortilla chips.

Chocolate and Peanut Butter Granola Clusters

If you follow me on Instagram, you'll know that chocolate and peanut butter are two of my favorite foods. So, when I pair them in this recipe, it brings me pure joy. You can enjoy the clusters on their own as a snack or serve with some milk (they make the milk taste fantastic). The chocolate chunks add that next level of deliciousness.

Yield: 6 servings

1½ cups (135 g) rolled oats, divided

¼ cup (30 g) cacao powder

½ tsp salt

¾ cup (90 g) walnuts, coarsely chopped

¾ cup (110 g) peanuts, coarsely chopped

1 tbsp (15 ml) maple syrup

¼ cup (60 ml) melted coconut oil

2 tsp (10 ml) vanilla extract

⅓ cup (85 g) smooth peanut butter, plus more for drizzling

⅓ cup (55 g) dark chocolate chips

Preheat the oven to 350°F (180°C or gas mark 4) and place a piece of parchment paper on a sheet pan.

In a large bowl, mix 1 cup (90 g) of the rolled oats with the cacao powder, salt, chopped walnuts and peanuts. In a high-speed blender or food processor, grind the remaining ½ cup (45 g) of rolled oats to create a flour. Add to the rolled oats mixture and stir to combine.

Add the maple syrup, coconut oil, vanilla extract and peanut butter. Combine and then fold in the dark chocolate chips. Use your hands to bring the mixture into a rough ball.

Place the ball onto the sheet pan and carefully flatten it until the granola is approximately ½-inch (1.3-cm) thick. Bake the slab of granola in the oven for 20 minutes.

Allow the granola to cool completely, then break it up with your hands or use a knife. Drizzle with extra peanut butter for serving.

Coffee and Walnut Scones

Scones are one of my favorite things to bake. This recipe only requires minimal kneading and you don't need to wait and let the dough to rise. You'll have the scones baking in the oven in under 20 minutes. Toasting the walnut crumbs on the sheet pan before folding through the scone mixture is an important step, as the flavor released from the walnuts is wonderful and paired with coffee makes them extra yummy. Don't forget the coffee icing drizzle either!

Yield: 8 scones

1 cup (115 g) walnuts, chopped into coarse crumbs

1 flax egg (1 tbsp [9 g] ground flaxseed + 2 tbsp [30 ml] water)

3 cups (375 g) all-purpose flour

2 tsp (9 g) baking powder

½ tsp ground cinnamon

¼ cup (55 g) light brown sugar

¾ cup (150 g) dairy-free butter, chilled

¼ cup (60 ml) full-fat coconut milk

2½ tbsp (40 ml) maple syrup

3 tsp (6 g) instant coffee granules, divided

1 cup (120 g) confectioners' sugar

Preheat the oven to 350°F (180°C or gas mark 4) and scatter the walnut crumbs onto a sheet pan. Place them in the oven to toast for 10 minutes.

Meanwhile, prepare the flax egg and set aside to soak for 5 minutes. In a large bowl, combine the flour, baking powder, cinnamon and brown sugar.

Add the butter and, using your hands, combine until a crumb-like mixture forms. Add the coconut milk, flax egg and maple syrup. Mix 2 teaspoons (4 g) of the instant coffee granules with 2 tablespoons (30 ml) of warm water and then add to the bowl. Stir together, then fold three-quarters of the toasted walnut crumbs into the mixture.

The mixture should now come together like a ball of dough. Transfer it to a work surface or chopping board and knead the dough for a minute. Flatten the ball so it is roughly 8 inches (20 cm) in diameter. Using a sharp knife, cut the circle in half, then each half into quarters to create eight triangles.

Place a piece of parchment paper on the sheet pan and carefully transfer the scones to the pan, ensuring there is space in between as they will rise. Bake them in the oven for 25 to 30 minutes.

While they're baking, prepare the icing by placing the remaining 1 teaspoon (2 g) of coffee granules into a bowl with 2 tablespoons (30 ml) of warm water. Add the confectioners' sugar and stir to combine.

Allow the scones to cool for 10 minutes, then drizzle the coffee icing over the scones and top them with the remaining toasted walnut crumbs. Serve warm.

Raspberry and White Chocolate Scones

I bet you've got most of these ingredients sitting in your kitchen cupboards to make another quick breakfast or even a snack/dessert recipe to bake in around 30 minutes. Your kitchen will smell delicious, and I bet you will demolish the whole batch by the end of the day. The white chocolate drizzle finishes them off perfectly.

Yield: 6–8 scones

1 flax egg (1 tbsp [9 g] ground flaxseed + 2 tbsp [30 ml] water)

3 cups (375 g) all-purpose flour, plus more for dusting

2 tsp (9 g) baking powder

⅓ cup (70 g) superfine/caster sugar

3¾ oz (150 g) dairy-free butter, chilled

¼ cup (60 ml) full-fat coconut milk

⅔ cup (110 g) dairy-free white chocolate chunks/chips, divided

⅓ cup (40 g) fresh raspberries, halved, divided

Preheat the oven to 350°F (180°C or gas mark 4). Line a sheet pan with parchment paper.

Prepare the flax egg and set it aside to soak for 5 minutes. In a large bowl, combine the flour, baking powder and sugar. Add the butter and, using your hands, combine until the mixture turns into crumbs. Add the flax egg and coconut milk and combine. Fold in 2 ounces (56 g) of the chocolate chunks.

Dust a little flour onto a work surface and place the dough on it. Set aside eight raspberry halves and add the rest of them to the top of the dough. Very gently knead the dough for a few seconds to distribute the raspberries more evenly throughout.

Shape the dough into a ball and carefully press down until it is roughly 8 inches (20 cm) in diameter. Using a cookie or circular cutter, cut out six to eight circles from the dough and place them onto the parchment-lined sheet pan. Leave some space between the scones so they can rise.

Poke the remaining raspberry halves on top along with about 1 ounce (27 g) of the remaining white chocolate chunks. Place the pan in the oven and bake for 25 minutes.

When ready to serve, melt the remaining white chocolate chunks in a microwave-safe bowl, microwaving in 30-second increments and stirring between. It should take 1 to 2 minutes for the chocolate to melt. Allow the scones to cool for 10 minutes, then drizzle with the melted chocolate. Enjoy!

Gingerbread Grain-Free Granola

This recipe epitomizes the concept of a sheet pan recipe. Simply combine the ingredients and scatter onto the sheet pan and let the oven do the magic. Although it provides all the fall feels, this granola can be enjoyed all year round. I adore the flavor of the pecans, walnuts and hazelnuts once they've toasted in the oven.

Yield: 8 servings

1 tsp allspice

½ tsp ground nutmeg

2 tsp (6 g) ground cinnamon

1 tsp ground cloves

2 tsp (6 g) ground ginger

¼ tsp salt

½ cup (120 ml) maple syrup

¼ cup (60 ml) melted coconut oil

1½ cups (165 g) pecans, roughly chopped

1 cup (115 g) walnuts, roughly chopped

¾ cup (90 g) hazelnuts, chopped

¾ cup (110 g) raisins

½ cup (70 g) sunflower seeds

½ cup (70 g) pumpkin seeds

1 cup (90 g) dried coconut

Coconut yogurt

Fresh berries

Preheat the oven to 350°F (180°C or gas mark 4). Line a sheet pan with parchment paper.

In a large bowl, combine the allspice, nutmeg, cinnamon, cloves, ginger, salt, maple syrup and coconut oil.

Add the pecans, walnuts, hazelnuts, raisins, sunflower seeds, pumpkin seeds and dried coconut. Combine thoroughly and then scatter onto the parchment-lined sheet pan.

Bake the granola in the oven for 25 to 30 minutes, stirring halfway through. Allow the granola to cool and harden for 15 minutes before eating or storing in an airtight container. Serve with coconut yogurt and fresh berries.

Easy Peasy
Lunches

This chapter is going to change your life with some flavor combinations you might not have tried before, like the Jackfruit Fajitas with Avocado Hummus (page 35) and Shawarma Tempeh Wraps (page 43). There are also some classics adapted to be even faster and more delicious, like Loaded Homemade Nachos with Walnut "Meat" (page 44).

Inspiration can lack when it comes to plant-based lunches and dinners. I certainly found these meals the hardest to plan when I first adopted a vegan diet. Therefore, I wanted to have lots of quick and easy sheet pan recipes in this book packed with vibrant veggies, such as the Italian Veggie Sheet Bake (page 40), and some really feel-good meals, like the Cajun Loaded Fries (page 36).

My advice to all new vegans and to those who simply wish to add more veggie-based meals to their diets is always to find and get comfortable making four or five recipes you really enjoy, and they'll stand you in great stead.

Cashew Mozzarella Pizza

Here's another cashew cheese recipe (find the other on page 10), but this one results in a different texture with more elasticity thanks to the cornstarch. The cornmeal adds a little crisp to the crust but if you can't get hold of any, feel free to omit this step. A little labor of love is required in this one, but the result will be worth it and oh so rewarding. Note that heating up the sheet pan before cooking the dough is a must in this recipe.

Yield: 2 servings

Cashew Mozzarella

1½ cups (220 g) cashews

1 cup (240 ml) dairy-free milk

Juice from 1 lemon

2 tbsp (20 g) nutritional yeast

2 tbsp (20 g) cornstarch

½ tsp salt

2 tsp (10 g) miso paste

Pizza Dough

1 package (2 level tsp [7 g]) active dry yeast

½ cup (120 ml) warm water

2 cups + 1 tbsp (260 g) all-purpose flour

1 tsp + 1 tbsp (15 ml) extra virgin olive oil, plus more to grease the bowl, divided

½ tsp salt

3 tbsp (45 ml) dairy-free milk

Place the cashews in a bowl and cover them with boiling water. Let the cashews soak while you prepare the dough and let it rise.

While the cashews soak, prepare the dough. In a large bowl, combine the active dry yeast and warm water, and leave for a couple of minutes to allow the yeast to start bubbling. When the yeast is bubbling, add the flour, 1 teaspoon of the olive oil, salt and milk, and combine until the mixture comes together as a dough. Sprinkle some flour onto a work surface and knead the dough for 5 minutes. Grease a large, clean bowl with a small amount of olive oil and place the ball of dough in the bowl. Cover the bowl with a tea towel and place it in a warm place for 1 hour.

After the dough has been rising for about 50 minutes, you can start the cashew mozzarella. Drain the cashews and place them a high-speed blender along with the milk, lemon juice, nutritional yeast, cornstarch, salt and miso paste. Blend until completely smooth.

Preheat the oven to 480°F (250°C or gas mark 9) and add 1 tablespoon (15 ml) of olive oil to one large sheet pan. Place the pan in the oven to heat up.

While the oven is heating, pour the cashew sauce into a saucepan and place it over a low heat. Stir or whisk every couple of minutes while it thickens. It should become extremely thick and clump together.

(continued)

Cashew Mozzarella Pizza (Continued)

Toppings

⅔ cup (150 g) tomato paste/
puree

¼ cup (60 ml) water

1 clove garlic, crushed

½ tsp dried oregano

1 tbsp (10 g) cornmeal, divided

2 large tomatoes, thinly sliced

Fresh basil

While the sauce is thickening, sprinkle some flour onto a work surface again and punch the air out of the dough, which should have roughly doubled in size. Place the dough on the work surface and use a rolling pin to roll the dough out to your desired pizza shape. The dough should be ¼-inch (6-mm) thick.

In a small bowl, combine the tomato paste, water, garlic and oregano.

Very carefully remove the pan from the oven. Sprinkle the pan with ½ tablespoon (5 g) of cornmeal. Place the pizza base onto the sheet pan and cover with the tomato paste mixture. Sprinkle the remaining cornmeal on the crust of the pizza.

Add the sliced tomatoes and cashew mozzarella, in dollops. Place the pan in the oven and bake for 15 to 18 minutes. Serve with some fresh basil leaves on top and dunk the crusts into any remaining cashew mozzarella. Enjoy!

Crispy Asian Tofu Fajitas with Peanut Miso Slaw

Peanut-miso slaw: It may sound like a weird combination but trust me it is spectacular! So spectacular, in fact, that you won't ever go back to regular coleslaw. The tofu in this recipe crisps up beautifully on your trusty sheet pan. The crunch from the coleslaw and peanuts against the crispy tofu and soft avocado is a culinary delight.

Yield: 3–4 servings

Crispy Asian Tofu

2 tbsp (30 ml) soy sauce

2 tbsp (30 ml) sesame oil

½ tsp garlic granules

14 oz (400 g) extra-firm smoked tofu, cubed

1 tbsp (10 g) cornstarch

Peanut-Miso Slaw

2 tsp (10 g) miso paste

3 tbsp (45 ml) vegan mayonnaise

1 tbsp (15 ml) water

3 tbsp (45 g) smooth peanut butter

3 scallions, sliced

1 medium carrot, peeled and cut into thin strips

1¼ cups (90 g) red cabbage, finely shredded

1¼ cups (90 g) white cabbage, finely shredded

Garnishes

4 large wraps

1 large avocado, mashed

2 tbsp (15 g) edamame

2 tbsp (20 g) peanuts

Fresh cilantro

Preheat the oven to 350°F (180°C or gas mark 4).

On a sheet pan combine the soy sauce, sesame oil and garlic granules. Add the tofu cubes and evenly coat in the marinade. Leave to marinate for at least 5 minutes, or up to overnight in the fridge.

When you are ready to cook the tofu, sprinkle the cornstarch over the tofu and give the pan a shake until the tofu cubes are evenly covered. Bake in the oven for 25 minutes, turning the tofu over halfway through.

While the tofu is baking, prepare the coleslaw by combining the miso paste, mayonnaise, water and peanut butter in a bowl. Add the scallions, carrots and cabbage. Mix to combine.

When the tofu is cooked, prepare the wraps by spreading some avocado on each. Load each wrap up with coleslaw, then add the tofu chunks and top with edamame, peanuts and cilantro. Wrap up and enjoy.

*See image on page 28.

Jackfruit Fajitas with Avocado Hummus

This is the only recipe using jackfruit in the book, so I've made sure it has that extra "wow" factor. Jackfruit straight out of the tin is pretty tasteless, but what makes jackfruit special is its texture when shredded. It mimics pulled pork so well, and when you get the flavors right—like you will find in this recipe—it's really special. Served with a creamy avocado hummus, these fajitas can be enjoyed warm or cold.

Yield: 4 servings

2 tbsp (30 ml) soy sauce

1 tbsp + 2 tsp (25 ml) extra virgin olive oil, divided

½ tsp smoked paprika

½ tsp garlic granules

¼ tsp chili powder

½ tsp ground cumin

¼ tsp dried oregano

Pinch of salt

1 (15-oz [425-g]) can jackfruit, drained

1 white onion, thinly sliced

1 red bell pepper, thinly sliced

1 green pepper, thinly sliced

1 large avocado, mashed

2 tbsp (30 g) hummus

4 large wraps

Shredded lettuce

Lime wedges

Sliced scallions

Chili flakes

Preheat the oven to 350°F (180°C or gas mark 4). Line a sheet pan with parchment paper.

In a large bowl, combine the soy sauce, 1 tablespoon (15 ml) of the olive oil, smoked paprika, garlic granules, chili powder, cumin, oregano and a pinch of salt. Using two forks, shred the jackfruit and then add it to the bowl. Combine until the jackfruit is evenly coated.

Transfer the jackfruit to half of the parchment-lined sheet pan. On the other half, add the onion and pepper slices. Drizzle the veggies with 2 teaspoons (10 ml) of the olive oil and place the pan into the oven. Bake for 25 minutes.

Meanwhile, combine the avocado with the hummus and spread it onto the wraps. Add some lettuce, the jackfruit and veggies, and finish by squeezing over some lime juice and garnishing with scallions and chili flakes.

Cajun Loaded Fries

This recipe is perfect for a weekend lunch with friends. Minimal effort is required after a long week at work and there is no need for your stove. Both the fries and black beans are cooked on the same sheet pan, and I love that when you cook black beans in the oven, they pop open and the outsides crisp up. The toppings add tons of flavor and complement the Cajun seasoning.

Yield: 3–4 servings

3 lb (1.4 kg) white potatoes, cut into fries

2 tsp (10 g) Cajun seasoning

3 tbsp (45 ml) extra virgin olive oil

½ tsp salt

1 (15-oz [425-g]) can black beans, drained

3 tbsp (80 g) canned corn

2 medium tomatoes, diced

1 large avocado, diced

3 scallions, sliced

3 tbsp (45 ml) vegan sour cream

Sliced jalapeños

Fresh cilantro

Lime wedges

Preheat the oven to 350°F (180°C or gas mark 4).

To a large bowl, add the fries, Cajun seasoning, olive oil and salt. Place a lid on the bowl or a chopping board over the top and give the bowl a good shake to coat the fries evenly in the seasoning and oil. Scatter the fries onto a large sheet pan and place in the oven for 40 minutes, giving them a stir halfway through.

Remove the pan from the oven and scatter the black beans over the fries. Place the pan back into the oven for 10 minutes, until the black bean skins start to pop open.

Take the pan out of the oven and load up the nachos with corn first, then the tomatoes, avocado, scallions, sour cream, jalapeños and cilantro, then squeeze some lime juice over the top before serving.

Chipotle Tofu and Chickpea Tacos

This recipe is great to prepare in advance. Thanks to the sheet pan, the chickpeas will crisp up beautifully and give a lovely texture alongside the softer tofu chunks. Chipotle is one of my favorite flavors as it has a slight kick but is not too overpowering. This recipe can be enjoyed hot or cold and would be a great meal to take to work for lunch.

Yield: 3–4 servings

1 tsp chipotle paste

4 tbsp (60 ml) extra virgin olive oil

2 (8-oz [226-g]) blocks extra-firm smoked tofu, cut into strips

1 (15-oz [425-g]) can chickpeas, drained and rinsed

½ cup (120 ml) dairy-free sour cream

8 mini tortilla wraps

1 cup (75 g) shredded lettuce

½ cup (60 g) sliced radishes

1 large avocado, mashed

3 scallions, sliced

Preheat the oven to 350°F (180°C or gas mark 4).

On a sheet pan, combine the chipotle paste and olive oil. Then add the tofu strips and chickpeas, and carefully stir until they're evenly coated. Bake for 25 minutes, until the chickpeas are starting to crisp.

Remove the pan from the oven and spread the sour cream onto the tortilla wraps, and add lettuce, chipotle tofu strips and chickpeas. Top with the radishes, avocado and scallions. Enjoy!

Italian Veggie Sheet Bake

I've been making this dish almost every week for months. It's a great way to pack lots of veggies in (six different types, in fact) and the black olives and warm crusty chunks of bread are heavenly. This is more of a lunch dish, but you could easily add some chickpeas or your favorite bean to turn this into dinner. The base of the sauce is rich and jam-packed with flavor, so don't pass up this sheet pan delight.

Yield: 4 servings

1 zucchini, halved and sliced

2 eggplants, halved and sliced

1 red bell pepper, sliced

1 orange bell pepper, sliced

1 large or 2 small red onions, roughly chopped

2 tbsp (30 ml) extra virgin olive oil, divided

½ tsp salt, divided

2 (15-oz [425-g]) cans chopped tomatoes, with liquid

3 cloves garlic, crushed

1½ tsp (2 g) dried oregano, divided

1 tsp tomato paste

2 tbsp (30 ml) balsamic vinegar

½ cup (90 g) black olives

2 slices of bread of choice, torn into chunks

9 oz (255 g) vine or cherry tomatoes

Fresh basil

Preheat the oven to 350°F (180°C or gas mark 4) and scatter the zucchini, eggplant, peppers and onion pieces onto the sheet pan. Drizzle the vegetables with 1 tablespoon (15 ml) of the olive oil, season with ¼ teaspoon of the salt and place into the oven to bake for 20 minutes.

Meanwhile, in a bowl, combine the canned tomatoes, garlic, 1 teaspoon of the oregano, tomato paste, balsamic vinegar and black olives.

Put the bread chunks in a small bowl and drizzle with the remaining 1 tablespoon (15 ml) of oil and ½ teaspoon of oregano. Toss to combine.

After the veggies have baked for 20 minutes, remove the pan from the oven and pour the tomato mixture over the veggies. Use a spatula to coat the vegetables in the sauce and then place the vine or cherry tomatoes on top. Place the pan back into the oven to bake for 15 minutes.

Remove the pan from the oven and add the bread chunks to the pan. Return the pan to the oven to bake for a final 10 minutes, until the bread chunks have hardened and turned crispy. Garnish with fresh basil and serve.

Shawarma Tempeh Wraps

For those that have never heard of or eaten tempeh, it's from the same soybean family as tofu but it is a fermented version with a completely different texture. Just like tofu, it's great at absorbing marinades like this homemade shawarma mix. You can prepare the shawarma tempeh the day before and have it waiting in your fridge ready to be baked on your sheet pan.

Yield: 3–4 servings

1 tbsp (6 g) ground cumin

1 tbsp (6 g) ground coriander

1 tsp garlic granules

1 tsp paprika

½ tsp ground cinnamon

½ tsp black pepper

½ tsp ground cardamom

¼ tsp ground cloves

½ tsp salt

⅓ cup (80 ml) extra virgin olive oil

2½ cups (400 g) tempeh, cut into strips

¾ cup (180 ml) vegan sour cream

6 large wraps

Shredded lettuce

½ cucumber, sliced into ribbons

½ red onion, diced

1 cup (150 g) cherry tomatoes, halved

Fresh parsley

In a bowl, combine the cumin, coriander, garlic granules, paprika, cinnamon, black pepper, cardamom, cloves, salt and olive oil. Add the tempeh strips and coat them well with the marinade. Let the tempeh marinate for a minimum of 1 hour or up to 24 hours in the fridge.

When ready to cook the tempeh, preheat the oven to 350°F (180°C or gas mark 4) and line a large sheet pan with parchment paper. Place the tempeh strips on the pan and bake for 20 minutes, turning the strips over halfway through.

When you're ready to eat, spread the sour cream on the wraps. Then add the lettuce, cucumber, red onion, cherry tomatoes and the shawarma tempeh. Garnish with fresh parsley and enjoy.

Loaded Homemade Nachos with Walnut "Meat"

If you've got guests coming over or want to impress somebody in general, this is the ONE! I bet you'd never think of using walnuts to substitute for taco meat, right?! Feel free to cut corners and use store-bought tortilla chips but in my opinion homemade are so much better. I could eat this for breakfast, lunch and dinner without sharing. Let your guests or partner try and guess what the "meat" is made of—they will be amazed.

Yield: 3–4 servings

Chips

5 tortilla wraps

3 tbsp (45 ml) extra virgin olive oil

Walnut "Meat"

2 cups (230 g) walnuts

1 tbsp (15 g) tomato paste

½ cup (30 g) sun-dried tomatoes, finely diced

2 tbsp (30 ml) soy sauce

½ tsp miso paste

¼ tsp chili powder

¼ tsp smoked paprika

¼ tsp ground cumin

Toppings

½ cup (60 g) grated dairy-free Cheddar-style cheese, divided

¼ red onion, diced

½ green bell pepper, diced

1 tomato, diced

1 avocado, cut into small chunks

2 tbsp (35 g) salsa

2 tbsp (30 ml) vegan sour cream

Fresh cilantro

Preheat the oven to 350°F (180°C or gas mark 4) and line two large sheet pans with parchment paper. Cut each wrap into four strips and then cut diagonal lines into those strips to create triangle chip shapes. Don't worry if they're not perfect.

Place the tortilla pieces onto one of the sheet pans and, using a brush or your hands, brush/rub the oil onto both sides of every piece. Place the pan into the oven and bake for 16 minutes, carefully turning the chips over halfway through.

While the chips are cooking, prepare the walnut "meat." You can either chop the walnuts by hand or place them in a blender or food processor and blend until they're crumb-like. In a large bowl, combine the tomato paste, sun-dried tomatoes, soy sauce, miso paste, chili powder, paprika and cumin, then add the walnut crumbs and stir until evenly coated.

Scatter the walnut crumbs onto the other sheet pan and place in the oven to bake for 15 minutes.

When the walnut meat is cooked, add half of the grated cheese and place the pan back into the oven or under the grill for a few extra minutes, until the cheese is melted.

Carefully scatter the cooked walnut "meat" on top of the nachos, then add the red onion, green pepper, tomato and avocado. Finish by adding the remaining grated cheese and then dollop with the salsa and sour cream. Sprinkle with the fresh cilantro and serve.

Tandoori Tempeh with Sweet Potatoes

I'm very proud of this dish and I hope you'll love it as much as I do. The tandoori tempeh paired with the coconut raita is a thing of beauty, and I love how the sweet potato and other veggies are transformed by the flavors. This dish will be on your table in under 40 minutes from start to finish, and the leftovers taste gorgeous reheated on the days to follow.

Yield: 3–4 servings

Tandoori Tempeh

1 tsp ground turmeric

½ tsp ground cumin

½ tsp ground coriander

¼ tsp chili powder

½-inch (1.3-cm) piece fresh ginger, grated

2 cloves garlic, crushed

1 tsp tomato paste

1 tbsp (15 ml) maple syrup

3 tbsp (45 ml) dairy-free yogurt

1 tbsp (15 ml) extra virgin olive oil

¼ tsp salt

14 oz (400 g) tempeh, cubed or chopped into chunks

18 oz (500 g) sweet potato, skin left on and chopped into ¾-inch (2-cm) chunks

1 red onion, chopped into ¾-inch (2-cm) chunks

3.5 oz (100 g) asparagus spears

1 orange bell pepper, cut into ¾-inch (2-cm) chunks

Fresh cilantro

Chili flakes, optional

Coconut Raita

¾ cup (180 ml) coconut yogurt

1 cup (115 g) grated cucumber

Handful of fresh mint leaves

Preheat the oven to 350°F (180°C or gas mark 4).

In a large bowl, combine the turmeric, cumin, coriander, chili powder, ginger, garlic, tomato paste, maple syrup, yogurt, olive oil and salt. Add the tempeh and sweet potato chunks, and mix until they're evenly coated. Empty the bowl onto a sheet pan and add the red onion, asparagus and bell pepper. Give the pan a shake to coat the vegetables and then place it into the oven to bake for 30 minutes.

Meanwhile, in a medium bowl, stir together the coconut yogurt, cucumber and mint leaves.

When the tempeh and sweet potatoes are done, dollop with the raita and garnish with fresh cilantro and some chili flakes, if you wish.

Portobello Mushroom Tacos with Spicy Chipotle Coleslaw

The flavors in this recipe make the mushrooms taste almost meaty, and chipotle in the homemade coleslaw is the perfect addition. The sheet pan is used to transform the mushrooms in the oven and results in a much better outcome than pan frying. I could eat these every day of the week!

Yield: 3–4 servings

Portobello Mushrooms

2 tbsp (30 ml) extra virgin olive oil

2 tbsp (30 ml) soy sauce

1 tbsp (15 ml) liquid smoke, optional

½ tsp cayenne pepper

½ tsp oregano

½ tsp paprika

1 tsp cornstarch

1 tsp onion granules

1 tsp garlic granules

2½ cups (500 g) portobello mushrooms, sliced

Spicy Chipotle Coleslaw

4 tbsp (60 ml) vegan mayonnaise

Juice of ½ lemon

½ tsp chipotle paste

¼ cup (12 g) scallions, thinly sliced

¾ cup (70 g) red cabbage, finely shredded

¾ cup (70 g) white cabbage, finely shredded

½ red apple, thinly sliced or grated

1 cup (105 g) carrots, thinly sliced or grated

½ tbsp (1 g) fresh cilantro, finely chopped

Pinch of salt and pepper

Tacos

8 small tortilla wraps

2 avocados, mashed

Iceberg lettuce, shredded

1 tbsp (3 g) fresh chives, finely chopped

Lime wedges

Preheat the oven to 350°F (180°C or gas mark 4) and line a large sheet pan with parchment paper.

In a bowl, combine the olive oil, soy sauce, liquid smoke, if using, cayenne pepper, oregano, paprika, cornstarch, onion granules and garlic granules. Add the mushrooms and coat them evenly with the marinade mixture.

Transfer the mushrooms to the lined sheet pan and place the pan into the oven to bake for 20 minutes.

While the mushrooms bake, in a medium bowl, combine the mayonnaise, lemon juice, chipotle paste, scallions, cabbages, apple, carrots, cilantro and a pinch each of salt and pepper.

When the mushrooms are cooked, spread the tortilla wraps with the avocado, and top with the shredded lettuce, mushrooms and coleslaw. Garnish with the chopped chives and finish with a squeeze of lime.

Fast and Flavorful Dinners

The goal of this chapter is to transform your day-to-day life and make cooking dinner less of a chore at the end of a busy day. There are five recipes that include tofu in this chapter and each one will prove that if you season and cook tofu right, it can absolutely make a dish. For example, crumbling the tofu on the Crumbled Chorizo-Style Tofu Gnocchi Bake (page 52) not only adds delicious flavors, but a lovely texture as well. In contrast, in the Silken Tofu Sausage Pasta Bake with Kale (page 67), softer tofu is blended into a mouthwatering smooth and creamy sauce for the pasta.

Fear not, there are plenty of recipes here that don't contain tofu and will still make your taste buds tingle. Try the Butternut Squash and Mole Tacos (page 72) if you like a bit of heat and want a fun recipe to share with family or friends. I am certain that at least one of these recipes will become a staple dinner in your household.

Crumbled Chorizo-Style Tofu Gnocchi Bake

This dish is full of flavor and warmth. It can be enjoyed with a simple side salad or on its own. If you want a dish that is good for the soul, this is the one for you. And just wait until you discover that sheet pan gnocchi is way better than boiled!

Yield: 6 servings

1 tbsp (15 ml) liquid smoke, optional

1 tbsp (15 ml) extra virgin olive oil

3 tbsp (45 ml) soy sauce

1 tbsp (15 ml) apple cider vinegar

1 tbsp (15 ml) maple or agave syrup

2 tsp (5 g) smoked paprika

1 tsp garlic granules or powder

½ tsp onion powder

½ tsp chili powder

2 (8-oz [227-g]) blocks firm tofu (smoked flavor is recommended)

1 (15-oz [425-g]) can chopped tomatoes, with liquid

2 cloves garlic, crushed

1 tsp dried oregano

1 tbsp (15 g) tomato paste

½ cup (25 g) sun-dried tomatoes

1 red onion, cut into small chunks

5 cups (625 g) vegan gnocchi

1 cup (110 g) dairy-free mozzarella or cheese of choice, grated or sliced, divided

Fresh basil

In a bowl, combine the liquid smoke, if using, with the olive oil, soy sauce, apple cider vinegar, maple syrup, smoked paprika, garlic granules, onion powder and chili powder. Crumble the tofu into the marinade and stir until it's evenly coated. Set aside or place in the fridge until ready to cook.

Preheat the oven to 350°F (180°C or gas mark 4).

In a medium bowl, combine the chopped tomatoes with the garlic, oregano and tomato paste. Add the sun-dried tomatoes, onion and gnocchi. Stir thoroughly then scatter onto a sheet pan. Sprinkle or place half of the grated or sliced cheese on top, followed by the crumbled chorizo-style tofu. Top with the remaining cheese then place the pan into the oven to bake for 25 minutes. Serve with fresh basil.

Vegan Sheet Pan Paella

This dish proves just how versatile sheet pan cooking can be. No need to precook the rice, just make sure your sheet pan has a lip to avoid any spills. The rice will absorb all the liquid while in the oven and the top layer will crisp up and add a beautiful texture to the paella. The skins of the cannellini beans will pop open and crisp up, adding another gorgeous element of texture to your plate.

Yield: 4 servings

1 white onion, finely diced

1 red bell pepper, thinly sliced

1 tbsp (15 ml) extra virgin olive oil

1 (15-oz [425-g]) can cannellini beans, drained and rinsed

2 cups (400 g) paella/arborio rice

2 tsp (5 g) smoked paprika

Pinch of saffron

2 cloves garlic, crushed

½ tsp salt

3 cups (720 ml) vegetable stock, divided

½ cup (60 g) green beans, chopped

½ cup (70 g) fresh or frozen peas

Lemon wedges

Fresh flat-leaf parsley

Preheat the oven to 350°F (180°C or gas mark 4).

Place the onion and bell pepper on a half sheet pan (13 x 18 inch [33 x 45 cm]) with a lip. Drizzle the olive oil over the vegetables and place the pan in the oven to bake for 5 minutes.

Meanwhile, in a large bowl, stir the beans, rice, paprika, saffron, garlic and salt to combine, ensuring the beans and rice are evenly coated in the paprika.

Remove the pan from the oven and add the bean and rice mixture, spreading it evenly on the sheet pan. Pour 2 cups (480 ml) of the vegetable stock over the mixture and very carefully place the pan back into the oven, ensuring no liquid is spilled.

Bake for 15 minutes, then remove the pan from the oven and give the paella a stir. Add the green beans, peas and the remaining vegetable stock to the pan and place it back in the oven to bake for 10 more minutes. The rice will have absorbed all the stock, be cooked through and the top will be crispy.

Serve with a squeeze of lemon juice and fresh parsley. Enjoy!

Sesame-Miso Roasted Butternut Squash with Puy Lentils

This dish is bursting with flavor and goodness from the vegetables and lentils. The Puy lentils will absorb the marinade while they cook. Minimal effort is required with this one, and it's another great one for meal prep. We always have some cooked Puy lentils in our cupboards as they are so versatile, and they are perfect in this recipe. I am obsessed with the miso and sesame flavors in this dish. Feel free to use some flatbread or something similar to mop up any juices.

Yield: 3 servings

1 medium (14-oz [400-g]) butternut squash

2 small red onions, cut into chunks

2 large or 3 small (about 11 oz [300 g]) parsnips, quartered lengthways

2 tbsp (30 ml) extra virgin olive oil, divided

2 tbsp (30 ml) sesame oil

2 tbsp (30 ml) soy sauce

1 tbsp (17 g) miso paste

1 tbsp (15 ml) rice vinegar

3 cloves garlic, crushed

10 oz (300 g) cooked Puy lentils

4 scallions, sliced

½ red chili pepper, roughly chopped

Sesame seeds

Fresh cilantro

Preheat the oven to 350°F (180°C or gas mark 4).

Peel, seed and slice the butternut squash then cut each slice in half. Place the squash slices on a sheet pan along with the onion chunks and parsnips. Drizzle 1 tablespoon (15 ml) of the olive oil over the vegetables and place the pan into the oven to bake for 20 minutes.

Meanwhile, in a medium bowl, mix the remaining 1 tablespoon (15 ml) of olive oil, sesame oil, soy sauce, miso, rice vinegar and garlic, then add the cooked lentils and stir to combine.

Remove the sheet pan from the oven, add the lentils and give everything a stir. Place the sheet pan back into the oven to bake for 15 minutes.

To serve, garnish with the scallions, red chili, sesame seeds and fresh cilantro.

Eggplant and Chickpea Tray Bake with Harissa Yogurt

If you want to learn how to jazz up eggplant then stop here and make this recipe. Harissa is a popular flavor in our household and works so well with the balsamic flavors that you get from the cooked eggplant. This recipe showcases sheet pan cooking beautifully, and there is nothing easier than adding everything to the pan and letting it work its magic in the oven. Plus, it's another fabulous way of eating lots of veggies that aren't boiled and bland.

Yield: 3–4 servings

1 tsp paprika

½ tsp oregano

2 cloves garlic, crushed

½ tsp salt

2 tbsp (30 ml) balsamic vinegar

3 tbsp (45 ml) extra virgin olive oil

2 medium eggplants, cut into 1-inch (2.5-cm) chunks

2 (15-oz [425-g]) cans chickpeas, drained and rinsed

1 red onion, cut into chunks

1 yellow bell pepper, sliced

9 oz (250 g) tomatoes on the vine

⅓ cup (60 g) black olives, halved

½ cup (120 ml) dairy-free yogurt

1 tsp harissa paste

Fresh parsley

4 flatbreads, lightly toasted

Preheat the oven to 350°F (180°C or gas mark 4).

In a medium bowl, combine the paprika, oregano, garlic, salt, balsamic vinegar and olive oil. Add the eggplant chunks and stir to combine.

Scatter the eggplant chunks on the sheet pan and place in the oven to bake for 15 minutes. Meanwhile, place the chickpeas in the same bowl that you used for the eggplant and stir to coat the chickpeas with leftover spices.

Remove the pan from the oven, add the chickpeas, onion and bell pepper and give everything a stir. Add the tomatoes (left whole and on the vine) to the pan then place it back into the oven to bake for an additional 15 minutes.

Remove the pan from the oven and add the olives then place the tray back into the oven to bake for 5 more minutes.

While the vegetables are baking, in a small bowl, combine the yogurt with the harissa paste.

Remove the pan from the oven, add dollops of some of the harissa yogurt, saving the rest for serving. Garnish with the fresh parsley and serve with toasted flatbreads and the harissa yogurt.

Teriyaki Tofu and Broccolini

This is the perfect example of how to jazz up tofu and veggies. Though this is a one-pan book, I couldn't resist including an optional homemade teriyaki sauce for those who don't mind turning on the stove, but rest assured, this recipe works just as well with store-bought vegan teriyaki sauce. Using the sheet pan, the tofu and veggies cook to perfection, and the sheet pan method allows them to drink up the amazing sauce. Reserve some of the sauce to serve alongside the rice, or store it in a jar in the fridge and use within a month.

Yield: 3–4 servings

Optional Homemade Teriyaki Sauce

⅓ cup (70 g) light brown sugar

4 tbsp (60 ml) soy sauce

2 tbsp (30 ml) mirin

3 tbsp (45 ml) sesame oil

1 clove garlic, minced

1 tsp freshly grated ginger

1 tbsp (10 g) cornstarch

½ cup (120 ml) vegan teriyaki sauce, divided

1 lb (450 g) extra-firm tofu, cut into ¾-inch (2-cm) chunks

3.5 oz (100 g) asparagus spears (roughly 12 pieces)

7 oz (200 g) broccolini

3.5 oz (100 g) sugar snap peas

3 oz (85 g) edamame

Sesame seeds

3 scallions, sliced

Cooked white rice

Preheat the oven to 350°F (180°C or gas mark 4).

If making your own teriyaki, combine the brown sugar, soy sauce, mirin, sesame oil and ⅔ cup (160 ml) of water in a saucepan. Place over medium heat and stir until the sugar dissolves, then add the garlic and ginger.

In a small bowl, combine the cornstarch with 1½ tablespoons (23 ml) of water and stir well. When the mixture is smooth and well blended, add it to the saucepan and stir. Cook the sauce for an additional 6 to 8 minutes, stirring frequently, as the teriyaki sauce thickens. If it becomes too thick, loosen it up by adding more water, 1 tablespoon (15 ml) at a time.

Drain your tofu and use a tofu press or heavy pan to press your tofu for 10 minutes.

Add the tofu chunks, asparagus, broccolini and sugar snap peas to a sheet pan and pour about two-thirds of the teriyaki sauce on top. Combine so the tofu and veggies are evenly covered in the sauce, and then place the pan into the oven to bake for 20 minutes.

Add the edamame to the pan and give everything on the pan a good stir, then place the pan back in the oven to bake for 5 more minutes.

Garnish with the sesame seeds and sliced scallions, and serve with rice and the remaining teriyaki sauce, if desired.

Sheet Pan "Meatballs" and Greens

Vegan "meatballs" taste nicer by far when they've been cooked in the oven than on the stove, in my opinion. With help from the breadcrumbs that bind the ingredients, they also crisp up, giving them a gorgeous texture. Please choose the vegan ground beef that most closely resembles meat, as anything too dry or dehydrated won't come together into a ball as well. I use the brands Meatless Farm or Richmond.

Sesame oil is one of my favorite oils to cook with and creates the tastiest portion of greens to serve alongside the "meatballs." This is another great meal prep recipe too.

Yield: 4 servings

3 cloves garlic, crushed

2 tbsp (8 g) fresh parsley, finely chopped

4 scallions, finely sliced, plus extra to garnish

2 tsp (10 g) miso paste

¼ tsp salt

Pinch of pepper

3 tbsp (45 ml) sesame oil, divided

18 oz (500 g) vegan ground beef

¼ cup (25 g) breadcrumbs

¾ cup (80 g) green beans

6 oz (175 g) broccolini

1 cup (100 g) sugar snap peas

¼ tsp garlic granules

Cooked white rice

Spicy vegan mayonnaise

Sesame seeds

Preheat the oven to 350°F (180°C or gas mark 4). Line a sheet pan with parchment paper.

In a medium bowl, combine the garlic, parsley, scallions, miso paste, salt, pepper and 2 tablespoons (30 ml) of sesame oil. Then add the vegan ground beef and breadcrumbs and stir well to combine. Using your hands, form the mixture into approximately 16 balls and place them on the parchment-lined sheet pan. Place the pan in the oven and bake for 10 minutes.

Remove the pan from the oven and add the green beans, broccolini and sugar snap peas. (If there is not enough room on the pan, use a separate pan.) Drizzle the remaining 1 tablespoon (15 ml) of sesame oil over the vegetables then sprinkle on the garlic granules.

Turn the "meatballs" over and then place the pan(s) back into the oven for an additional 20 minutes. Serve with cooked white rice and spicy mayo. Garnish with additional sliced scallions and some sesame seeds.

Greek-Style Tacos with Dairy-Free Tzatziki and Feta Salad

Lima beans are one of my favorites and I think they are so underrated. Roasted on your sheet pan the skins pop open, giving them a crispy exterior and soft interior. With Greek flavors from the feta, olives and oregano these tacos are different from ordinary tacos and bound to be a crowd pleaser. Don't forget the tzatziki for another burst of flavor!

Yield: 3–4 servings

Tacos

1 (15-oz [425-g]) can lima beans, drained and rinsed

2 tbsp (30ml) extra virgin olive oil, divided

1 tsp dried oregano

½ red onion, diced

¼ cucumber, diced

1 large tomato, diced

⅓ cup (60 g) black olives, halved

¾ cup (115 g) dairy-free feta chunks

8 mini tortilla wraps

Tzatziki

½ cup (120 ml) dairy-free coconut yogurt

¼ cucumber, grated, liquid squeezed out

1 tbsp (6 g) fresh mint, chopped

Preheat the oven to 350°F (180°C or gas mark 4).

Scatter the lima beans on a sheet pan. Drizzle the beans with 1 tablespoon (30 ml) of the olive oil and sprinkle with the oregano. Gently shake the pan until the beans are evenly coated. Place the pan in the oven and bake for 25 minutes, until the lima beans are crispy on the outside and the skins have popped open.

Meanwhile, prepare the Greek salad in a medium bowl by combining the onion, cucumber, tomato, olives and feta chunks.

To make the tzatziki, combine the yogurt, grated cucumber and chopped mint in a small bowl.

Warm the wraps, if you wish.

To assemble the tacos, scoop the lima beans onto the wraps, add the feta salad and top with tzatziki. Enjoy!

Silken Tofu Sausage Pasta Bake with Kale

This recipe does require an additional pot, but I promise it is worth it! This recipe is so good that I just had to include it in my sheet pan book.

The beauty of sheet pan cooking is the large surface area the pan provides. In this recipe it results in a gorgeous crispy top on the pasta bake. Silken tofu is my hero product in so many sweet and savory recipes. It adds smoothness to sauces and is a great way of adding protein to a veggie/vegan dish. Use your favorite meat-free sausages, and you can use penne pasta instead of the fusilli. Ground nutmeg is a must in the sauce here, so don't skip it. You'll find yourself wanting a second serving of this pasta bake so you may want to keep this dish to yourself!

Yield: 4–6 servings

¾ cup (100 g) chopped cashews

6 vegan sausages

1 lb (450 g) dried fusilli pasta

1 white onion, roughly diced

1 tbsp (15 ml) extra virgin olive oil

2 cloves garlic, crushed

3 cups (210 g) white mushrooms, sliced

¾ cup (85 g) dairy-free shredded cheese plus 1 more handful for topping

¾ cup (180 ml) dairy-free milk

¼ tsp ground nutmeg

½ tsp salt

1 tbsp (15 ml) soy sauce

2 tbsp (10 g) nutritional yeast

1⅓ cups (300 g) silken tofu

1 cup (70 g) kale, chopped

2 tbsp (15 g) breadcrumbs

2 tbsp (6 g) fresh chives, diced

Cover the cashews in boiling water and leave them to soak for 30 minutes. After 15 minutes, preheat the oven to 350°F (180°C or gas mark 4).

Place the sausages on a sheet pan and into the oven for half of the cooking time recommended on the package.

Cook the pasta according to the package instructions. While the pasta is cooking, remove the sausages from the oven and set aside. On the same sheet pan, add the onion and drizzle with olive oil. Bake for about 5 minutes, then add the garlic and mushrooms.

Meanwhile, add the shredded cheese, milk, nutmeg, salt, soy sauce, nutritional yeast and silken tofu to a blender. Drain the cashews, add them to the blender then blend until completely smooth.

Cut the cooked sausages into quarters. Add them to the pan with the mushrooms and kale and cook for a few minutes, until the kale has begun to wilt.

Drain the cooked pasta and add it to the pan with the rest of the ingredients along with the sauce. Combine well before transferring to a sheet pan.

Sprinkle the breadcrumbs on top, along with a handful of grated cheese. Place the pan in the oven to bake for 15 minutes. Serve topped with the chives.

Baked Tofu Buddha Tray

Standard Buddha bowls will be a thing of the past once you use your sheet pan to cook the ingredients. Minimal washing up makes this recipe a go-to for those evenings when you've had a long day and can't be bothered to cook. With the help from the oil, the outer edges of the red cabbage will crisp up nicely, yet the inside will be soft. The red cabbage chunks will fall apart in your mouth. Roasted red cabbage is a favorite vegetable and the paprika smoked tofu chunks with a dollop of hummus are delightful. This is a perfect prep recipe to ensure you're feeding your body plenty of goodness even on a busy day.

Yield: 3–4 servings

4 tbsp (60 ml) extra virgin olive oil, divided

1 tsp smoked paprika

½ tsp onion granules

1 lb (450 g) smoked tofu, cut into ¾-inch (2-cm) chunks

1 red bell pepper, sliced

5 oz (150 g) broccolini

¼ head red cabbage, cut into chunks

½ head cauliflower, cut into florets

Hummus

Pinch of chili flakes

Preheat the oven to 350°F (180°C or gas mark 4).

In a large bowl, combine 3 tablespoons (45 ml) of the olive oil with the smoked paprika and onion granules. Add the tofu chunks and stir gently to coat them evenly in the marinade.

Scatter the tofu on the left-hand side of a sheet pan then add the bell pepper, broccolini, cabbage and cauliflower to the right-hand side. Drizzle the remaining 1 tablespoon (15 ml) of olive oil over the vegetables and place the pan into the oven to bake for 30 minutes.

Serve with hummus and some chili flakes on the tofu, if you wish.

Peanut Tofu Steaks

This dish is a version of a meal I made all the time when I transitioned to a plant-based diet. Learning to marinate tofu is a game changer, as most will agree that plain tofu has little to no flavor. This marinade has a slight kick, but the peanut sauce complements it beautifully. You'll want to drink any leftover sauce straight from the bowl.

Yield: 3 servings

Tofu Steaks

2 tbsp + 1 tsp (35 ml) sesame oil, divided

2 tbsp (30 ml) soy sauce

1 tsp cayenne pepper

½ tsp chili paste

½ tsp garlic granules

1 lb (450 g) extra-firm tofu, sliced and cut in half diagonally

1 white onion, sliced

1 red bell pepper, sliced

1 orange bell pepper, sliced

Cooked white rice

Sliced scallions

Crushed peanuts

Peanut Sauce

⅓ cup (85 g) smooth peanut butter

2 tbsp (30 ml) soy sauce

1 tsp chili paste

⅓ cup (80 ml) boiling water

Preheat the oven to 350°F (180°C or gas mark 4).

Drain your tofu and use a tofu press or heavy pan to press your tofu for 10 minutes.

In a medium bowl, combine 2 tablespoons (30 ml) of the sesame oil, the soy sauce, cayenne pepper, chili paste and garlic granules. Coat the tofu steaks evenly with the marinade then place them on one half of a sheet pan.

Place the onion and bell peppers on the other half of the pan. Drizzle the veggies with the remaining 1 teaspoon of sesame oil then place the sheet pan into the oven to bake for 25 minutes.

About 5 minutes before tofu and veggies will be finished, in a medium bowl whisk the peanut butter, soy sauce, chili paste and boiling water to combine.

Serve the baked tofu and vegetables alongside cooked white rice, drizzled with the peanut sauce. Garnish with the sliced scallions and crushed peanuts.

Butternut Squash and Mole Tacos

If you like tacos with a bit of heat to them, these are for you. The homemade mole sauce combined with black beans caramelizes into pure deliciousness.

Yield: 3–4 servings

**Optional Homemade
Black Bean Mole Sauce**

0.5 oz (15 g) dried chipotle chilies

1 tsp extra virgin olive oil

½ white onion, diced

2 cloves garlic, crushed

½ tsp dried oregano

½ tsp ground cumin

1 tsp tomato paste

½ tsp cacao powder

⅓ cup + 2 tsp (90 ml) vegetable stock

¼ tsp salt

1 (15-oz [425-g]) can black beans, drained

Roasted Squash

1 lb (450 g) butternut squash chunks

2 tbsp (30 ml) extra virgin olive oil

Salt, to season

½ white onion, sliced

½ cup (120 ml) store-bought or homemade mole sauce

8 mini tortilla wraps

1 large avocado, cut into small chunks

½ cup (75 g) dairy-free feta

3 scallions, sliced

Preheat the oven to 350°F (180°C or gas mark 4).

If you are making your own mole, slice the chipotle chilies in half, scrape out all the seeds and remove the stems. Place the chilies in a bowl and cover them with boiling water, then let them soak for 15 minutes.

Scatter the butternut squash chunks on half of a sheet pan, drizzle the chunks with the olive oil and give the pan a shake to ensure the squash is evenly coated in the oil. Season with salt and place in the oven to bake for 20 minutes.

While the squash is roasting, prepare the sauce. Heat a pan over medium heat and add the olive oil and diced onion. Cook until the onion turns translucent, about 5 minutes, then add the garlic, oregano, cumin, tomato paste and cacao powder. Stir well and cook for 3 minutes more.

Drain the rehydrated chilies and add them to a high-speed blender along with the vegetable stock, salt and cooked onion mixture. Blend until completely smooth.

Take the pan out of the oven and add the sliced onion on top of the butternut squash. Stir the black beans into the mole sauce and then transfer the mixture to the other half of the sheet pan.

Place the sheet pan back into the oven for 12 to 15 minutes, until the sliced onion is cooked and the black bean mix is heated through.

Load up the mini tortilla wraps with the cooked squash and black bean mole sauce.

Top with avocado chunks, crumbled feta and scallions. Enjoy!

Maple-Glazed Sausages and Veggies

This is a gorgeously sweet and sticky sausage dish brimming with flavor. The cooked sliced apples paired with the hints of rosemary are so tasty. It's another "chuck-it-on-a-pan-and-roast" recipe—our favorite kind, right?! Serve with your favorite greens (mine is broccolini).

Yield: 3–4 servings

1¾ cups (350 g) cubed butternut squash

1 red bell pepper, sliced

1 red onion, cut into chunks

1 zucchini, sliced and halved

1 tbsp (15 ml) extra virgin olive oil, plus extra for drizzling

2 tbsp (30 ml) maple syrup

1 tbsp (15 ml) balsamic vinegar

¼ tsp Dijon mustard

Pinch of salt and pepper

8 vegan sausages

1 Royal Gala apple, cut into chunks

1 sprig fresh rosemary

Cooked broccolini

Fresh bread

Preheat the oven to 350°F (180°C or gas mark 4).

On a sheet pan scatter the squash, bell pepper, onion and zucchini. Drizzle some olive oil over the veggies, toss to coat and place in the oven to bake for 10 minutes.

In a small bowl, combine the olive oil, maple syrup, balsamic vinegar, mustard and a pinch of salt and pepper.

Take the pan out of the oven and add the vegan sausages and apple chunks to the pan. Pour the marinade over everything on the sheet pan. Give the pan a good shake to make sure the vegetables are coated in the liquid. Sprinkle the rosemary over the pan and place the pan back into the oven to bake for 20 minutes, until the sausages are cooked and the apple chunks are soft.

Serve with the broccolini and fresh bread.

Speedy Savory Snacks and Sides

Whether you're off to a picnic, entertaining guests with a buffet or simply want to make a couple of these recipes and combine them for lunch or dinner, these will not disappoint. You don't need any fancy gadgets or equipment to make these recipes. Simply cook and serve on your sheet pan!

The Miso-Butter Smashed Potatoes (page 102) need only seven ingredients and take just 45 minutes. They will hands down be the tastiest potatoes you have ever eaten. The umami flavors from the miso paste paired with butter is a match made in heaven.

I am a big snacker. Snacks are good for the soul. And homemade ones are way better than store bought, in my opinion. My Teriyaki Mushroom and Potato Filo Parcels (page 104) are better than anything you can find in a store. If we are going to a gathering with family or friends, I am known for bringing my still-warm Pesto Sausage Rolls (page 98). I remember taking them to a gathering with my girlfriends and them saying they were hands down better than any sausage rolls they'd ever eaten. Now that's a compliment, right?! You are bound to find a recipe in this chapter that will become your new go-to.

Bow Tie Pasta Crisps and Dips

This is one of two pasta recipes in the book I couldn't do without. You will need a second pan to boil the pasta but you're going to love the result!

A TikTok trend that went viral, these are a fabulous alternative for chips/crisps. If you're home and fancying chips/crisps and there's nothing in the cupboard but pasta, look no further—I've got your back. Any pasta shape will work but farfalle is great for scooping up the dips. With three dips to choose from, there will always be a free dip to scoop from!

Yield: 4–6 servings

Pasta Crisps

1 lb (450 g) farfalle pasta

3 tbsp (45 ml) extra virgin olive oil

1 tsp paprika

1 tsp dried oregano

⅓ cup (30 g) dairy-free Parmesan

¼ tsp salt

Sour Cream Dip

1 cup (240 ml) vegan sour cream

3 tbsp (10 g) fresh chives, finely chopped

½ tsp garlic granules

½ tsp onion granules

Guacamole

1 large avocado, mashed

¼ red onion, diced

2 tbsp (2 g) fresh cilantro, diced

Juice from ½ lime

½ red chili pepper, diced

½ clove garlic, crushed

Salsa

1 (15-oz [425-g]) can diced tomatoes with liquid

¼ red onion, diced

2 jalapeño peppers, diced

Juice from ½ lime

½ clove garlic, crushed

2 tbsp (2 g) fresh cilantro, diced

Heat a large pan of water over medium heat and once boiling, add the pasta. Cook for 12 minutes then drain and rinse with cold water.

While the pasta is cooking, preheat the oven to 350°F (180°C or gas mark 4).

In a medium bowl, combine the cooked pasta, olive oil, paprika, oregano and dairy-free Parmesan. Scatter the pasta onto a large sheet pan and place in the oven to bake for 35 to 40 minutes, or until they are hard and crisp.

Prepare the dips while the pasta is in the oven. Simply combine the ingredients for each in three separate bowls. If you want the salsa to be less chunky, add the diced tomatoes to a blender or food processor and blend for a few seconds before combining with the rest of the salsa ingredients.

Allow the pasta crisps to cool for 10 minutes before sprinkling with the salt and enjoying by dunking the chips in the dips!

Homemade Seeded Crackers

These crackers are goodness in a bite. Packed with tons of nutritional benefits from the different seeds, they couldn't be easier to make. You can taste the rosemary flavor in each mouthful, and you could use dried oregano instead if you prefer. Serve these crackers with your favorite dip (mine is hummus) and pack these for your work snacks. They'll keep you satisfied between meals and give your brain all the energy it needs to get you through the day.

Yield: 8–10 crackers

¾ cup (105 g) pumpkin seeds/pepitas

½ cup (100 g) sunflower seeds

¼ cup (40 g) chia seeds

2 tbsp (20 g) sesame seeds

3 tbsp (30 g) ground flaxseed

2 tbsp (30 g) hemp seeds

½ tsp salt

2 tsp (4 g) dried rosemary

1 cup (240 ml) lukewarm water

Hummus or dip of choice

In a large bowl, combine the pumpkin seeds, sunflower seeds, chia seeds, sesame seeds, ground flaxseed, hemp seeds, salt, rosemary and water and leave the bowl to rest for 20 minutes. Meanwhile, preheat the oven to 325°F (165°C or gas mark 3) and line a half sheet pan (13 x 18 inch [33 x 45 cm]) with parchment paper.

After the mixture has soaked for 20 minutes, transfer it to the parchment-covered pan and carefully spread the dough until it reaches all corners. Bake in the oven for 45 to 50 minutes, or until the crackers are hard, taking it out of the oven halfway through to cut into your desired cracker shapes.

Allow the crackers to cool for 10 minutes before serving with hummus or your dip of choice.

Mini Tomato and Cheese Puff Pastry Tarts

This is the ultimate party-pleasing recipe. You can even prepare these tarts in advance and keep them in the fridge until you're ready to cook them. They are best eaten warm so you can enjoy the gooey melted cheese. And you could even use a smoked version of the cheese to enhance the flavors. The flakiness of the pastry against the melted cheese and cooked tomatoes is to die for!

Yield: 6 tarts

1⅔ cups (250 g) multicolored tomatoes on the vine, halved

1 clove garlic, crushed

⅛ tsp salt

1 tbsp (15 ml) extra virgin olive oil, divided

1 sheet store-bought vegan puff pastry

6 slices vegan cheese

½ tbsp (8 ml) soy sauce

Fresh basil

Pine nuts

Preheat the oven to 350°F (180°C or gas mark 4).

In a medium bowl, combine the tomatoes, garlic, salt and ½ tablespoon (8 ml) of the olive oil.

Roll out the puff pastry sheet and cut it into six squares. Transfer the squares onto a sheet pan.

Score a square within each piece of pastry approximately ½ inch (1.3 cm) from the edge. Place a slice of vegan cheese within each of the inner squares. You may need to trim off the edges of the slice of cheese to make it fit. Top each piece of cheese with some tomatoes.

In a small bowl, combine the remaining olive oil and the soy sauce. Use a brush or your finger to wash the mixture on the outer edges of the puff pastry.

Place the pans into the oven to bake for 25 minutes, until the edges have risen and are golden brown. Top with fresh basil and sprinkle with some pine nuts. Enjoy!

Roasted Rainbow Veggies with Turmeric Tahini

This is the perfect dish to show that you can make any veggie amazing when there is something tasty to drizzle over or dip them in, like this turmeric tahini. There are five portions of vegetables here, which is fabulous, and they can all roast at the same time as long as you make sure the butternut squash chunks are small enough so they cook in time. This is a fabulous side dish, but you could also add a can of chickpeas or similar beans to make it a main meal.

Yield: 4 servings

Rainbow Veggies

2 red bell peppers, sliced into large chunks

2 yellow bell peppers, sliced into large chunks

1 head of broccoli, chopped into florets

1 medium (14-oz [400-g]) butternut squash, cut into 1-inch (2.5-cm) cubes

2 red onions, cut into chunks

3 tbsp (45 ml) extra virgin olive oil

1 tbsp (15 ml) soy sauce

½ tsp salt

½ tsp onion granules

Turmeric Tahini

½ cup (120 ml) tahini

1 clove garlic, crushed

¾ tsp ground turmeric

1 tbsp (15 ml) extra virgin olive oil

1 tbsp (15 ml) lemon juice

1 tbsp (15 ml) maple syrup

Sesame seeds, optional

Preheat the oven to oven to 350°F (180°C or gas mark 4).

Arrange the veggies on a sheet pan starting with the red peppers followed by the yellow peppers, then broccoli, squash and red onions.

In a small bowl, combine the olive oil, soy sauce, salt and onion granules then drizzle over the vegetables. Give the pan a shake, then place it into the oven to bake for 30 minutes.

Meanwhile, prepare the dressing in a medium bowl by combining the tahini, garlic, turmeric, olive oil, lemon juice and maple syrup. When the vegetables are cooked, drizzle them with the tahini and sprinkle with some sesame seeds, if you wish.

Rosemary Roasted Almonds and Pumpkin Seeds

If you're having guests and want to put out some nibbles before serving main dishes, then these beautifully roasted rosemary nuts and seeds are just what you need. They also make a tasty snack to munch on throughout the day. Garlic and rosemary work great together and these beauties take just 20 minutes to make.

Yield: 10 servings

2 tbsp (30 ml) extra virgin olive oil

2 tbsp (4 g) fresh rosemary, finely chopped

½ tsp garlic granules

½ tsp salt, plus more for sprinkling

2 cups (285 g) whole almonds

⅓ cup (45 g) pumpkin seeds

Preheat the oven to 350°F (180°C or gas mark 4).

In a medium bowl, combine the olive oil, rosemary, garlic granules and salt. Add the almonds and coat them evenly in the oil mixture. Scoop the almonds out of the bowl, saving the bowl with the oil and spices. Scatter the almonds on a sheet pan and place the pan into the oven to bake for 12 minutes.

While the almonds are roasting, add the pumpkin seeds to the bowl you used to mix the almonds and coat the seeds in the excess oil and spices. After the almonds have baked for 12 minutes, carefully remove the sheet pan from the oven and add the pumpkin seeds to the pan. Give the almonds a shake to incorporate the pumpkin seeds then place the pan back into the oven to bake for 8 more minutes.

Allow the almonds and pumpkin seeds to cool slightly before adding an extra pinch of salt and devouring them.

Red Cabbage Steaks with Olive Tapenade and Cream Cheese

Roasted red cabbage is simply glorious. Cabbages are one of the cheapest vegetables and are so versatile—from eating it raw in a coleslaw to enjoying it slow roasted with a tapenade that is brimming with flavor alongside cream cheese. The capers add a salty element to this recipe, which works nicely with the cheese. This is a super quick and simple side dish that will ensure you are eating some goodness.

Yield: 6 servings

Cabbage Steaks

1 large or 2 small red cabbages, sliced into ¾-inch (2-cm) "steaks"

1 tbsp (15 ml) extra virgin olive oil

Pinch of salt

2 tbsp (30 g) dairy-free cream cheese

Fresh parsley

Olive Tapenade

½ cup (90 g) black olives, pits removed and diced

1 tbsp (15 ml) extra virgin olive oil

½ tsp capers, chopped

2 cloves garlic, crushed

1 tbsp (15 ml) lemon juice

½ tbsp (2 g) fresh parsley, chopped

Preheat the oven to 350°F (180°C or gas mark 4).

Place the red cabbage steaks onto a sheet pan. Drizzle with the olive oil, season with the salt and place in the oven to roast for 25 to 30 minutes.

Meanwhile, in a small bowl stir together the olives, olive oil, capers, garlic, lemon juice and chopped parsley.

When the cabbage has finished roasting, spread some cream cheese on top of each steak then add the olive tapenade. Garnish with some fresh parsley.

Stuffed Hasselback Sweet Potatoes with Coconut Bacon

Coconut bacon: yes, you heard that right! With a little helping hand from our trusty sheet pan, coconut flakes are transformed and given a gorgeous smoky flavor thanks to the marinade. Hasselback potatoes are one of my favorites, as I love that the slices get nice and crispy in the oven. White potatoes are most commonly hasselback'd, but try this with sweet potatoes and they're even yummier. Be careful not to slice through the whole potato when making the cuts. Placing the potatoes on a wooden spoon as you slice should help stop this.

Yield: 6 servings

Sweet Potatoes

28 oz (1.25 kg) sweet potatoes

1 tbsp (15 ml) extra virgin olive oil

½ cup (60 g) dairy-free grated Cheddar-style cheese

½ cup (120 ml) dairy-free sour cream

1 tbsp (3 g) fresh chives, chopped

Coconut Bacon

½ tbsp (8 ml) liquid smoke

½ tbsp (8 ml) soy sauce or tamari

½ tbsp (8 ml) maple syrup

½ tsp smoked paprika

Pinch of salt

1 cup (45 g) coconut flakes

Preheat the oven to 350°F (180°C or gas mark 4).

Place a sweet potato onto a wooden spoon and using a knife, carefully cut down through three-quarters of the potato. Repeat, cutting lines thinly spaced through the whole potato, making sure you don't cut all the way through. Rub the potatoes in the olive oil and place on a sheet pan. Put the pan into the oven to bake for 35 to 40 minutes.

While the potatoes bake, combine the liquid smoke, soy sauce, maple syrup, paprika and a pinch of salt. Add the coconut flakes and stir to coat them in the marinade. Scatter them on a small sheet pan.

Place the sheet pan into the oven when the potatoes have about 10 minutes left to bake. Remove the pan with the potatoes from the oven and sprinkle them with the grated cheese then place the pan back into the oven for the remaining 10 minutes.

When the potatoes and bacon have baked for the remaining 10 minutes, remove both pans from the oven and top the potatoes with the sour cream, coconut bacon and a sprinkle of fresh chives.

Crispy Roasted Chickpeas

These are a quick and easy crispy snack you can prepare on a Sunday and munch through your busy week. High in protein and fiber, they'll help to satisfy your hunger, and adding the cayenne pepper will give them a spicy kick. Removing the skins will make them crispier but if you're in too much of a rush feel free to leave the skins on. I'm sure you already have most if not all of the ingredients at home, so whip these up and give them a try. The trick is to spread them out on the sheet pan so every edge can crisp up.

Yield: 6 servings

2 (15-oz [425-g]) cans chickpeas, drained and rinsed

2 tbsp (30 ml) extra virgin olive oil

½ tsp cayenne pepper

1 tsp paprika

½ tsp ground cumin

½ tsp salt

1 tsp fresh parsley, chopped

Pinch of chili flakes, optional

Preheat the oven to 350°F (180°C or gas mark 4).

Scatter the chickpeas onto one half of a tea towel, fold the other half on top and very gently rub the chickpeas. This will remove some of their skins. Using your hands remove the rest of the skins and place the chickpeas into a medium bowl.

In a separate small bowl, combine the olive oil, cayenne pepper, paprika, cumin and salt. Drizzle the mixture over the chickpeas and toss carefully to combine.

Scatter the chickpeas onto a sheet pan and place in the oven to bake for 40 to 45 minutes, turning halfway. Allow them to cool slightly before garnishing with some fresh parsley and some chili flakes, if you wish.

Homemade Vegan Parmesan Roasted Broccoli

Have you ever made your own vegan Parmesan? It's a lot easier than you might think and gets its cheesy flavor from nutritional yeast, which is a staple ingredient in our house. Using almonds and cashews to create the texture, this Parmesan is packed with protein and jazzes up any veggie. Broccoli works well with it, and you can have the florets roasting and crisping up on your sheet pan in the oven while you prepare the Parmesan. These quantities will yield lots of leftover Parmesan, so store it in a jar and sprinkle on other meals as you please. I enjoy this dish as an afternoon snack, but you can rustle it up as a delicious side dish too.

Yield: 4–6 servings

2 heads of broccoli, cut into florets

2 tbsp (30 ml) extra virgin olive oil

1 tsp salt, plus more for seasoning the broccoli

4 tbsp (20 g) nutritional yeast

¾ cup (110 g) almonds

½ cup (65 g) cashews

¾ tsp garlic granules

Preheat the oven to 350°F (180°C or gas mark 4).

Scatter the broccoli florets onto a sheet pan and drizzle with the olive oil. Season with a pinch of salt and place the pan into the oven to bake for 25 minutes.

While the broccoli is roasting, prepare the vegan Parmesan by placing the nutritional yeast, almonds, cashews, garlic granules and salt in a blender. Blend until coarse crumbs form.

At the end of the baking time, remove the broccoli from the oven and immediately sprinkle it with some of the Parmesan.

Greek-Style Focaccia

I think one of the best flavors in the world is extra virgin olive oil. And this focaccia puts olive oil front and center. With the olives, dairy-free feta and rosemary to add a Greek twist, you will be slicing this straight out of the oven as the gorgeous smells take over your kitchen. Using a sheet pan gives a large surface area, meaning more focaccia. Even better!

Yield: 9–12 servings

2½ tsp (10 g) fast-acting instant dried yeast

1½ cup (360 ml) warm water

3¼ cups (445 g) white bread flour

1½ tsp (9 g) salt

4 tbsp (60 ml) extra virgin olive oil, divided, plus more for the pan

½ cup (90 g) black olives

2 sprigs (2 tbsp [3 g]) fresh rosemary

½ cup (75 g) dairy-free feta, crumbled

In a large bowl, combine the yeast and warm water. Set aside for a few minutes to allow the yeast to bubble.

When the yeast is bubbling, add the bread flour and salt and, using your hands, combine the ingredients. Add 2 tablespoons (30 ml) of the olive oil and bring the mixture together into a dough.

Sprinkle some flour onto a work surface and knead the dough for 3 minutes. Clean the bowl you mixed the bread in, then grease it with a tiny drizzle of oil. Place the kneaded dough into the bowl, cover it with a tea towel and put the bowl in a warm place for 1 hour, or until doubled in size.

Grease a half sheet pan (13 x 18 inch [33 x 45 cm]) with a drizzle of olive oil. Transfer the dough in the sheet pan and gently stretch it into all four corners. Place the tea towel back over the pan and place the pan back into a warm place for 30 minutes.

Preheat the oven to 350°F (180°C or gas mark 4).

Use your fingers to poke some holes into the dough. Place the olives in the holes then drizzle the dough with the remaining 2 tablespoons (30 ml) of olive oil.

Push the rosemary sprigs into the surface of the dough then place the pan in the oven to bake for 20 to 25 minutes, until a toothpick inserted into the focaccia comes out clean.

Allow the focaccia to cool slightly before crumbling the feta over it, cutting into pieces and serving.

Pesto Sausage Rolls

This is a combination you might not have tried, but pesto in a sausage roll is simply incredible. I've made mini sausage rolls in this recipe but feel free to make larger ones, if you wish—they'll just need an extra 5 minutes in the oven. Make sure you spread them out on the sheet pan, as they'll rise as the puff pastry cooks. These are best eaten warm straight of the oven. You really won't want to share these!

Yield: 18 mini rolls

1 sheet store-bought vegan puff pastry

3 tbsp (45 g) vegan green pesto

14 oz (400 g) vegan sausage meat

1 tbsp (15 ml) soy sauce

1 tbsp (15 ml) maple syrup

1 tsp sesame seeds

Preheat the oven to 350°F (180°C or gas mark 4). Line a sheet pan with a piece of parchment paper.

Unroll the sheet of puff pastry onto a work surface with the pastry laid out horizontally. Cut the pastry into thirds and then spread 1 tablespoon (15 g) of the pesto on the left-hand side of each piece down the whole length of each strip.

Remove the skins from the sausages and crumble the meat into a bowl. Scatter the crumbled sausage on top of the pesto.

Carefully fold the right-hand side of the pastry over the left, sealing the edges together with a fork.

Cut each log into six pieces and transfer them to the parchment-lined sheet pan.

In a small bowl, combine the soy sauce and maple syrup then brush it over each sausage roll. Sprinkle the sesame seeds on top of the rolls and place the pan in the oven to bake for 20 to 25 minutes.

Roasted Root Vegetables with Satay Sauce

You'd never think to put root vegetables with satay sauce but boy does this pairing work. Root vegetables are some of the cheapest in supermarkets, and this combination with the sweet parsnips against the nutty, umami sauce is magnificent. Keeping the skins on for extra fiber and to save time preparing, this dish is a case of simply placing all the veggie chunks onto your loyal sheet pan and letting the magic happen in the oven.

Yield: 4–6 servings

Roasted Veggies

10.5 oz (300 g) parsnips

12 oz (350 g) carrots

21 oz (600 g) sweet potato

2 red onions

2 tbsp (30 ml) extra virgin olive oil

½ tsp salt

Pinch of pepper

Fresh cilantro

Peanuts

Chili flakes, optional

Satay Sauce

½ cup (130 g) smooth peanut butter

½ (15-oz [445-ml]) can full-fat coconut milk

2 tbsp (30 ml) soy sauce or tamari

1 tsp mild curry powder

½ tsp light brown sugar

Preheat the oven to 350°F (180°C or gas mark 4).

Cut the parsnips, carrots, sweet potatoes and onions into chunks of a similar size, leaving the skins on. Scatter them onto a sheet pan and drizzle the olive oil over all the veggies. Season with the salt and pepper and place in the oven to bake for 45 minutes.

Meanwhile, prepare the sauce. Add the peanut butter, coconut milk, soy sauce, curry powder and brown sugar to a microwave-safe bowl. Microwave in 30-second intervals, gently stirring in between intervals, until the sauce is smooth and at your desire temperature.

Serve the sauce alongside the cooked vegetables. Garnish with fresh cilantro, peanuts and chili flakes, if you wish.

Miso-Butter Smashed Potatoes

These potatoes will, without a doubt, be the most delicious potatoes you ever eat. Smashing them onto the sheet pan allows them to crisp up to perfection. And don't forget the miso butter, which couldn't be easier to prepare. I can assure you that you'll have eaten several before you've even served them to your loved ones, so I'd recommend doubling the ingredients to make an extra big batch. They even taste amazing cold!

Yield: 6 servings

4.5 lb (2 kg) baby/new potatoes

½ cup (115 g) dairy-free butter

1½ tbsp (26 g) miso paste

2 cloves garlic, crushed

3 scallions, sliced

1 tsp sesame seeds

Fresh cilantro

Poke each potato with a fork a few times to allow steam to release while cooking. Cook the potatoes in the microwave for 10 minutes or until the potatoes are soft enough to smash. Set aside.

Preheat the oven to 350°F (180°C or gas mark 4).

Melt the butter in the microwave then stir in the miso and garlic until smooth. Depending on thickness of the miso paste (all store-bought ones are different) you may need to put the whole mixture back in the microwave for 10 to 15 seconds to soften the miso paste in order for it to combine.

Using a potato masher or fork, smash each potato so they break. Drizzle them with the miso butter and use a spoon or spatula to make sure they are completely coated.

Place the pan in the oven and roast for 25 minutes. When cooked, garnish with the sliced scallions, sesame seeds and fresh cilantro.

Teriyaki Mushroom and Potato Filo Parcels

These parcels are what everybody needs at their party. You can prepare the filling well in advance as it needs time in the fridge to cool, so you won't be frantically rushing to make them on the day of the party. Though this is a one-pan book, I couldn't resist including an optional homemade teriyaki sauce for those who don't mind turning on the stove, but rest assured, this recipe works just as well with store-bought vegan teriyaki sauce. The homemade teriyaki sauce is stress-free to make, and the quantities allow you to keep half for dunking the parcels in upon serving.

Yield: 12 servings

Mushroom and Potato Parcels

4¼ cups (300 g) white mushrooms, diced

1⅔ cups (250 g) new potatoes, diced

3 scallions, sliced, plus more to garnish

1 tbsp (15 ml) extra virgin olive oil

½ tsp salt

6 sheets vegan filo pastry

¼ cup (60 ml) vegan butter, melted)

½ cup (120 ml) store-bought teriyaki sauce

Optional Homemade Teriyaki Sauce

½ cup (110 g) light brown sugar

4 tbsp (60 ml) soy sauce

2 tbsp (30 ml) mirin

2 tbsp (30 ml) sesame oil

2 cloves garlic, crushed

1 tsp freshly grated ginger

2 tsp (5 g) cornstarch

Preheat the oven to 350°F (180°C or gas mark 4). Toss the mushrooms, potatoes and scallions with the olive oil and salt. Place them on a sheet pan and bake for 15 minutes.

While the mushrooms and potatoes are cooking, prepare the sauce if making. In a medium saucepan, combine the brown sugar, soy sauce, mirin, sesame oil, garlic and ginger. Place the pan over medium heat and stir as the sauce starts to bubble, cooking approximately 5 minutes. While the sauce cooks, in a small bowl, combine the cornstarch with 2 tablespoons (30 ml) of water. Stir until the cornstarch mixture is smooth then add it to the sauce and stir well to combine. The sauce will start to thicken within a couple of minutes. Stir frequently as it thickens. Once thick, take the sauce off the heat and put to one side.

When the potatoes are cooked and soft, dump that mixture into a bowl along with half of the teriyaki sauce. Reserve the other half of the teriyaki sauce for serving. (It can be stored at room temperature until serving.)

Place the veggie and teriyaki sauce mixture in the fridge for approximately 1 hour. This will allow the mixture to thicken slightly and the sauce to solidify.

Line a sheet pan with parchment paper.

Lay out the sheets of filo pastry on top of one another and cut a line down the middle from one short side to the other. Fold one half back up and place a damp tea towel over the sheets to keep them from drying out.

Next, take one sheet of filo pastry and drizzle it with some of the melted butter. Add 1 tablespoon (15 g) of the cooled mushroom mix to one end of the pastry strip, leaving the edges uncovered. Now fold both opposite ends over as if you're wrapping a burrito. Roll the parcel all the way up. The ends should be secure from the first two folds.

Repeat with the rest of the mixture and 11 remaining rectangles of pastry. Place the rolls onto the parchment-lined sheet pan and brush them with the remaining melted butter. Bake in for 20 to 25 minutes, until they are crispy and golden brown.

Serve with the remaining teriyaki sauce. If it has thickened too much to dip the parcels in, add some hot water and stir to loosen. Garnish the parcels with any additional sliced scallions.

*See photo on page 76.

Sweet Sheet Pan Delights

Desserts are nicer than most people. They don't cause drama or let you down. You can count on them to always be there (if you put your apron on and get baking, that is). These are foolproof sweet recipes that require no fancy skills. There are nutty, fruity, chocolatey and many more delightfully flavored recipes in this chapter. These bakes are the ultimate gifts to share with loved ones. Freeze or refrigerate the dough for Dark Chocolate and Marshmallow Cookies (page 112) or Giant Sheet Cookies (page 119) so you can enjoy a fresh cookie or two each evening, or double the quantities to make big batches to drop off to your neighbors or serve up at parties.

Although lacking egg and dairy, these certainly don't lack on flavor or the texture we long for in these baked goods. My aim is to prove that plant-based desserts don't lack in flavor or substance, and I hope this chapter cements that and leaves you with a long list of things to make. My advice is to make an oat milk latte to enjoy alongside whichever bake you choose to make, and enjoy both in some peace and quiet while savoring every mouthful and slurp (my definition of self-care).

Carrot Sheet Cake

I couldn't not include a carrot sheet cake in this book. I am obsessed with the flavors you get from the combination of spices in this sheet cake. It might look like there are a lot of ingredients, but I'm confident that you'll already have most of them in your pantry. The ratio of cream cheese frosting to carrot cake is pretty much even due to the thinness of the cake. This makes it way better than a standard, deeper sheet cake. You can never have too much cream cheese frosting, right?!

Yield: 12 servings

½ cup (110 g) dairy-free butter

2¼ cups (520 g) dairy-free cream cheese

1⅔ cups (200 g) confectioners' sugar

¼ cup (30 g) cornstarch

3 cups (375 g) all-purpose flour

⅔ cup (60 g) oatmeal

2½ (7 g) tsp ground cinnamon

¾ tsp ground nutmeg

½ tsp ground ginger

1 cup (220 g) light brown sugar

1½ tsp (7 g) baking powder

1¼ cups (300 ml) dairy-free milk

1 tbsp (15 ml) vanilla extract

3 tbsp (45 ml) maple syrup

3⅔ cups (400 g) shredded carrot

1½ cups (180 g) crushed walnuts, divided

⅓ cup (50 g) raisins

Preheat the oven to 350°F (180°C or gas mark 4). Line a rimmed half sheet pan (13 x 18 inch [33 x 45 cm]) with parchment paper.

Prepare the frosting first to allow enough time for it to chill so it will set. To a medium bowl, add the butter and cream cheese. Use an electric mixer to combine the two until creamy. Add the confectioners' sugar slowly while continuing to mix. When combined, add the cornstarch and mix for another minute. The frosting should not be runny. Place the bowl in the fridge to set while you make the batter and bake the cake.

In a large bowl, combine the flour, oatmeal, cinnamon, nutmeg, ginger, brown sugar and baking powder.

In a separate bowl combine the milk, vanilla and maple syrup. Pour the wet ingredients into the dry ingredients and stir to combine then fold in the carrots, 1 cup (120 g) of the walnuts and the raisins. Transfer the batter to the parchment-lined sheet pan. Smooth the batter into the corners, then place the pan into the oven to bake for 20 to 25 minutes, or until a toothpick or skewer inserted into the cake comes out cleanly.

Let the cake cool for 10 minutes before spreading with the cream cheese frosting. Sprinkle the remaining walnuts over the cake, slice and enjoy.

Strawberry Galette

This is a simple galette recipe with minimal ingredients or fuss—the best type of recipe. Use fresh or frozen sliced strawberries. Just note that it'll need a couple of minutes more in the oven if you're using frozen. Top with sliced almonds or coconut flakes and enjoy on its own, or with a scoop of dairy-free vanilla ice cream or custard. It's like a hug in a bowl!

The secret to a good galette is using your hands to make sure the flour and butter are thoroughly combined—then don't forget to chill it in the fridge.

Yield: 6 servings

1½ cups (200 g) all-purpose flour, plus more for rolling

½ tsp salt

½ cup (100 g) dairy-free butter, chilled

3 tbsp (45 ml) ice cold water

1½ cups (240 g) fresh or frozen strawberries, sliced

2 tbsp (30 g) granulated sugar

1 tbsp (15 ml) lemon juice

1 tbsp (15 ml) maple syrup

Almond or coconut flakes

Dairy-free ice cream

Combine the flour and salt in a large bowl. Add the butter and, using your hands, combine the ingredients until crumbs form.

Add the cold water, 1 tablespoon (15 ml) at a time, and continue to mix until the crumbs form a dough. Cover the bowl and place the dough in the refrigerator for 1 hour to chill.

Preheat the oven to 350°F (180°C or gas mark 4) and line a sheet pan with parchment paper.

Sprinkle some flour onto a work surface and using a rolling pin roll the chilled mixture out to approximately the size of a dinner plate. Place a dinner plate on top of the pastry and cut around it to get a perfectly round shape. Transfer the pastry carefully onto the sheet pan.

In a medium bowl, combine the strawberries with the sugar and lemon juice. Arrange the sliced strawberries in the center of the pastry, leaving a 1-inch (2.5-cm) gap around the edge.

Fold the edges of the pastry over the strawberries and pinch them as you go until all the edges are folded inward. Brush the maple syrup over the pastry then place the sheet pan into the oven to bake for 25 minutes, or until the pastry is golden.

Allow the galette to cool for 5 minutes before sprinkling with the sliced almonds or coconut flakes. Slice and enjoy with a scoop of ice cream, if you wish.

Dark Chocolate and Marshmallow Cookies

My most popular recipes are always ones that involve cookies, and if you've not tried marshmallows in your cookies, this recipe will blow your mind. With melted chocolate chips and gooey marshmallow, you'll be reaching for a second cookie before you've finished your first.

Yield: 10 servings

½ cup (100 g) dairy-free butter, chilled

½ cup (110 g) light brown sugar

⅓ cup (80 g) smooth applesauce

1 tsp baking powder

1½ cups (200 g) all-purpose flour

2 tsp (10 ml) vanilla extract

½ cup (80 g) dark chocolate chips/chunks, divided

⅔ cup (30 g) vegan mini marshmallows, divided

Preheat the oven to 350°F (180°C or gas mark 4). Line one large sheet pan with parchment paper.

To a large bowl, add the dairy-free butter, brown sugar and applesauce, and using a hand or electric whisk, cream for 30 seconds.

Add the baking powder, flour and vanilla and use a large spoon to combine. Fold in three-quarters of the chocolate chips and mini marshmallows.

Using a tablespoon or scoop, form ten balls of the dough and spread them out on the parchment-lined sheet pan.

Flatten the balls slightly then push the remaining chocolate chips and mini marshmallows into them. Place the pan in the oven to bake for 15 minutes. Allow them to cool and harden for 5 minutes before eating. Enjoy!

Peanut Butter and Jam Brownies

These sheet pan brownies are a match made in heaven. Not only do they bake in half the time of a standard brownie, but the ratio of PB and J to brownie is almost equal, meaning every mouthful is packed with chocolate-y gooeyness. You could even swap the peanut butter for almond butter—just make sure it's smooth and runny so you can make the pretty swirls.

Yield: 12 servings

1¼ cups (150 g) frozen raspberries

1¼ cups (150 g) all-purpose flour

¾ tsp baking powder

½ cup (45 g) cacao powder

½ cup (110 g) light brown sugar

1¼ cups (210 g) dark chocolate chips, melted

¼ cup (60 ml) dairy-free butter, melted

1¾ cups (420 ml) dairy-free milk (at room temperature)

1 tsp vanilla extract

⅔ cup (170 g) smooth, runny peanut butter, divided

⅓ cup (60 g) fresh raspberries, halved

1 tbsp (10 g) peanuts, halved

Preheat the oven to 350°F (180°C or gas mark 4) and place a piece of parchment paper on a half sheet pan (13 x 18 inch [33 x 45 cm]).

Place the frozen raspberries in a microwave-safe bowl and microwave in 30-second intervals until they are thawed and have released their juices. Mash until smooth.

In a large bowl, combine the flour, baking powder, cacao powder and brown sugar. In a separate bowl, combine the melted dark chocolate and butter, room-temperature milk, vanilla and ⅓ cup (85 g) of the peanut butter.

Pour the wet mixture into the dry and stir well, then transfer the batter to the parchment-lined sheet pan. Push the mixture into the corners.

Carefully mash the thawed raspberries with a potato masher or fork. Spoon the raspberries on top of the brownie mixture in lines, from one of the longest sides of the pan to the other.

Repeat with the remaining half of the peanut butter so it's spread just underneath each mashed raspberry line.

Use a knife or skewer to make lines from one short side to the other and then repeat in the opposite direction to create the swirls. Top with the halved fresh raspberries and peanut halves and place the pan in the oven to bake for 15 to 20 minutes, or until firm but still a bit gooey inside.

Allow the brownies to cool for 10 minutes before cutting into portions. Enjoy.

Yogurt Bark

This recipe is a fun one to make, so get the kids involved and they can enjoy this yogurt bark as a healthy snack or dessert. The advantage of using a sheet pan here, rather than something like a chopping board, is that the pan gets cold super quick in the freezer, meaning the bark will start to set immediately.

Yield: 10 pieces

3½ cups (820 ml) coconut yogurt

¼ cup (30 g) cacao powder

2 tbsp (30 ml) maple syrup

½ cup (75 g) fresh strawberries, sliced

½ cup (60 g) fresh raspberries, halved

¼ cup (30 g) chopped hazelnuts

2 tbsp (15 g) cacao nibs

1 tbsp (10 g) coconut flakes

Line a sheet pan with parchment paper.

In a large bowl, stir the yogurt, cacao powder and maple syrup until the cacao powder is well mixed throughout the yogurt.

Transfer the yogurt mixture to the parchment-lined pan and using a spatula or flat knife, smooth until the yogurt is flat and even.

Push the strawberries and raspberries into the yogurt and scatter the hazelnuts, cacao nibs and coconut flakes on top.

Place in the freezer for 2 hours, then cut into pieces and enjoy. Store leftovers in the freezer.

Giant Sheet Cookie

Say goodbye to that cookie scoop, this cookie sheet requires a lot less effort to make. You will need a half sheet pan (13 x 18 inch [33 x 45 cm]) at least ½-inch (1.3-cm) deep (the cookies will rise, hence the minimum depth required). I decorated the cookie in thirds with the toppings, but feel free to add them however you wish. The giant cookie is crispy on top but chewy underneath, just how every cookie should be.

Yield: 12 servings

1 cup (200 g) dairy-free butter, spread form recommended

⅔ cup (145 g) light brown sugar

⅔ cup (130 g) superfine sugar

1 tbsp (15 ml) vanilla extract

¼ cup (60 ml) dairy-free milk

1½ tsp (7 g) baking powder

2½ cups (350 g) all-purpose flour

¼ tsp salt

2 tbsp (20 g) dark chocolate chips

5 Oreos® (cut into quarters)

1 handful pretzels

Preheat the oven to 350°F (180°C or gas mark 4) and line a half sheet pan (13 x 18 inch [33 x 45 cm]) with a piece of parchment paper.

To a large bowl, add the butter, brown sugar and superfine sugar. Use an electric mixture to cream the ingredients, then add the vanilla and milk and mix again. Add the baking powder, flour and salt and use a large spoon or spatula combine. Transfer the ingredients to the parchment-lined sheet pan and flatten the mixture out until it reaches all four corners of the pan.

Cover one-third of the pan with dark chocolate chips, another third with Oreo quarters and the last with pretzels. Place the sheet pan in the oven to bake for 20 minutes.

Allow the giant cookie to cool for 15 minutes before slicing and enjoying warm.

Salted Caramel and Pecan Blondies

Sheet pan desserts like these blondies are the perfect crowd pleaser and double up as a thoughtful gift. Though this is a one-pan book, I couldn't resist including an optional homemade caramel sauce but store-bought works well too! The salted caramel makes them gooey and moist, especially as it seeps through the blondies as they bake—and don't forget the extra drizzle before serving!

Yield: 12 blondies

Salted Caramel

1 cup (220 g) light brown sugar

1 (15-oz [445-ml]) can full-fat coconut milk

1½ tsp (9 g) salt

Pecan Blondies

½ cup (120 ml) vegan salted caramel

1¼ cups (300 ml) dairy-free plain yogurt

3 tbsp (45 ml) maple syrup

1 cup (220 g) light brown sugar

1½ cups (190 g) all-purpose flour

1½ tsp (7 g) baking powder

⅔ cup (110 g) dairy-free white chocolate chunks, divided

1 cup (110 g) pecans, divided

If you are making your own caramel, combine the brown sugar and coconut milk in a large saucepan over medium heat. Stirring occasionally, bring the mixture to the boil for a few minutes then turn the heat down. Stir every couple of minutes while it thickens and turns to caramel. This will take 12 to 15 minutes. When it has darkened and become smooth enough to drizzle, add the salt and stir well, and then place the pan off the heat to cool down.

Preheat the oven to 350°F (180°C or gas mark 4) and line a half sheet pan (13 x 18 inch [33 x 45 cm]) with parchment paper.

In a large bowl, stir the yogurt, maple syrup and brown sugar until the sugar has dissolved, then add the flour and baking powder and stir well.

Fold in three-quarters of the white chocolate chunks and pecans then transfer the mixture to the sheet pan. Spread the mixture into the four corners and then using roughly 6 tablespoons (90 ml) of the salted caramel, drizzle it in lines over the batter.

Top with the remaining white chocolate and pecans and place in the oven to bake for 18 to 20 minutes, or until a skewer or knife comes out clean when inserted into the blondie. Allow the blondies to cool for 20 minutes, then drizzle with the extra salted caramel, slice and enjoy.

Nutty Brownies

This is a fail-safe recipe for gloriously gooey brownies. The flavor of the coffee granules is very subtle but works beautifully with the chocolate and nuts. Although they're thinner because of the sheet pan, they don't lose any moisture thanks to the chewy chopped dates scattered throughout that melt in the oven. Because they're thin, they're not too rich, so in my opinion it's perfectly acceptable to eat another.

Yield: 12 brownies

1½ cups (190 g) all-purpose flour

1 tsp baking powder

½ cup (45 g) cacao powder

½ cup (110 g) light brown sugar

1¼ cups (210 g) dark chocolate chips, melted

¾ cup (110 g) pitted, chopped dates

1½ cups (360 ml) dairy-free milk (at room temperature)

½ cup (130 g) cashew butter

1 tbsp (5 g) instant coffee granules

½ cup (70 g) chopped almonds, divided

½ cup (75 g) cashews, divided

½ cup (55 g) chopped pecans, divided

Dairy-free vanilla ice cream, optional

Preheat the oven to 350°F (180°C or gas mark 4) and place a piece of parchment paper on a half sheet pan (13 x 18 inch [33 x 45 cm]).

In a medium bowl, combine the flour, baking powder, cacao powder and brown sugar. In a large bowl, combine the melted chocolate, dates, milk and cashew butter. In a small bowl, combine the coffee granules with 1 tablespoon (15 ml) of warm water and once the coffee has dissolved, add it to the bowl with the wet ingredients and stir until smooth.

Pour the dry ingredients into the wet ingredients and combine, then fold in half of the chopped almonds, cashews and pecans. Transfer the mixture to the sheet pan and using a spatula carefully spread it into the corners and ensure it's nice and even.

Sprinkle the remaining nuts all over the mixture and place the pan into the oven to bake for 15 to 20 minutes, or until firm but still a bit gooey inside. Allow to cool for 5 to 10 minutes before slicing. Enjoy alone or with some dairy-free vanilla ice cream.

Almond and Hazelnut Biscotti

Your sheet pan will be needed three times in this recipe: to toast the nuts and to twice bake these gorgeous biscuits. Most famously served alongside coffee, biscotti have the perfect crunch and are great for dunking. Toasting the nuts at the beginning will bring out their flavors, and I love that you can taste both the nuts separately in every mouthful. I recommend drizzling the dark chocolate over and eating them within 24 hours while they maintain the crunch!

Yield: 14–16 biscotti

½ cup (60 g) chopped hazelnuts

½ cup (70 g) sliced almonds

⅓ cup (75 g) dairy-free butter

⅔ cup (130 g) superfine sugar

1 tsp vanilla extract

¼ cup (60 ml) dairy-free milk, plus more if needed

½ cup (50 g) ground almonds

½ tsp salt

1½ cups (190 g) all-purpose flour

½ tsp baking powder

2 tbsp (20 g) dark chocolate chips, melted, optional

Preheat the oven to 350°F (180°C or gas mark 4).

Scatter the chopped hazelnuts and sliced almonds onto a sheet pan and place in the oven to toast for 5 minutes.

In a bowl, cream the butter and sugar using a hand or electric whisk. Add the vanilla extract and milk and whisk again until combined.

Add the ground almonds, salt, flour and baking powder and stir to combine, then fold in the toasted chopped hazelnuts and almonds. The mixture should come together to form a dough. If it looks too dry and crumbly add more milk, 1 tablespoon (15 ml) at a time.

Place the ball of dough onto the sheet pan and roughly divide in two. Form two logs of dough approximately 2½ to 3 inches (6 to 8 cm) wide. Make sure there is plenty of space between the two logs.

Place the sheet pan in the oven to bake for 20 minutes then remove and allow the dough to cool completely. When cool, slice horizontally into the biscotti and place the slices back onto the tray with one of the inside sides facing up.

Preheat the oven again (if you have turned it off) then bake for 5 minutes. Carefully turn the biscotti over and bake on the other side for another 5 minutes.

If desired, drizzle with some melted dark chocolate to decorate.

White Chocolate and Raspberry Sheet Blondies

The popular duo of white chocolate and raspberries work beautifully together due to the sweetness of the chocolate and sourness of the berries. These blondies are dense and gooey, just how a blondie should be. The mixture will seem thin as you spread it in the sheet pan but don't worry, as it will rise as it bakes. Only taking half the time to bake than a standard blondie due to the large surface area of the sheet pan, these blondies will be ready to eat pretty much after you've washed up and put the kettle on.

Yield: 12 blondies

½ cup (110 g) dairy-free butter

1¼ cups (110 g) dairy-free white chocolate chips, divided

1¼ cups (275 g) light brown sugar

¾ cup (180 ml) dairy-free plain yogurt

1 tsp vanilla extract

½ tsp salt

1 tsp baking powder

2 cups (250 g) all-purpose flour

1 cup (125 g) fresh or frozen raspberries, divided

Preheat the oven to 350°F (180°C or gas mark 4). Line a half sheet pan (13 x 18 inch [33 x 45 cm]) with parchment paper.

In the microwave, melt the butter and ¼ cup (22 g) of the white chocolate chips and stir to combine. Add the brown sugar, yogurt and vanilla and stir to combine. Add the salt, baking powder and flour and combine until the mixture is smooth.

Fold three-quarters of the raspberries and ¾ cup (66 g) of the chocolate chips carefully into the mixture then transfer the batter to the parchment-lined sheet pan.

Carefully spread the mixture into all four corners. Sprinkle the remaining raspberries and remaining ¼ cup (22 g) of the chocolate chips on top. Place the sheet pan in the oven to bake for 15 minutes, or until a toothpick inserted in the brownies comes out clean, then allow to cool before slicing in the pan.

Chocolate Hazelnut Puff Pastry Twists

This is a bold statement, but this may be one of my favorite recipes to date. With minimal ingredients and a little help from your blender to make the chocolate hazelnut spread, these twists are super fun to make, and the result is the perfect accompaniment with your morning or afternoon coffee. Don't forget to add salt to the spread and to toast the hazelnuts first, as both will help heighten the flavors. The twisting of the puffs can get a little messy but it's worth it for the pretty masterpiece at the end.

Yield: 10–12 twists

Chocolate Hazelnut Spread

2½ cups (290 g) hazelnuts

⅔ cup (110 g) dark chocolate chips or chunks

1 tbsp (15 ml) vanilla extract

½ tsp salt

Puff Pastry Twists

2 sheets store-bought puff pastry

2 tbsp (30 ml) maple syrup

2 tbsp (15 g) crushed hazelnuts

Preheat the oven to 350°F (180°C or gas mark 4).

Scatter the whole hazelnuts onto a sheet pan. Place the pan into the oven to toast for 10 minutes. Allow the hazelnuts to cool slightly before removing most of the skins from the nuts. You can rub them between a tea towel, or another trick is to place them into a tin or plastic container and shake vigorously.

When most of the skins have been removed, place the toasted hazelnuts into a high-speed blender and blend until butter forms. You may need to scrape down the sides of the blender a few times. Depending on the power of your blender it may take between 3 to 15 minutes until a smooth runny nut butter is formed.

Meanwhile, melt the chocolate in the microwave and once the nut butter is runny add the chocolate to the blender along with the vanilla extract and salt. Blend until combined.

Roll out one sheet of puff pastry and spread roughly 2½ tablespoons (40 ml) of the chocolate hazelnut spread over the sheet, leaving a ¼-inch (6-mm) gap around the edge. Roll the sheet back up from one longest side to the other.

Place the log onto the sheet pan and using a sharp knife, cut a line vertically from one end to the other. Seal the two pieces at the top and then carefully twist the two pieces around each other before sealing at the other end using your fingers. Brush the maple syrup over the pastry and sprinkle with the crushed hazelnuts.

Repeat with the other sheet of puff pastry and ensure there is space between the two twists before placing the pan into the oven to bake for 30 minutes. Cut each twist into five or six pieces to serve.

Sheet Pan Apple Crisp

Once you've made an apple crisp (or crumble, as we call it in the UK) on a sheet pan, you won't want to make it any other way. Using the pan means the ratio of apple to crisp is 50/50, so this one is for the topping lovers. The recipe yields a big batch so it will feed plenty. It's best served immediately with custard or ice cream.

Yield: 6 servings

½ cup (110 g) dairy-free butter, plus more for greasing

⅓ cup (70 g) superfine sugar

1 tsp ground cinnamon

1 tbsp (15 ml) vanilla extract

7 Royal Gala apples, cored and sliced

⅓ cup (75 g) light brown sugar

⅔ cup (75 g) pecans, finely chopped

½ cup (60 g) all-purpose flour

2 cups (180 g) oats

1 tbsp (10 g) cornstarch

¼ tsp salt

2 tbsp (30 ml) maple syrup

Dairy-free custard or ice cream

Preheat the oven to 350°F (180°C or gas mark 4) and grease a half sheet pan (13 x 18 inch [33 x 45 cm]) with dairy-free butter.

In a large bowl, combine the superfine sugar, cinnamon and vanilla. Add the apple slices and toss in the bowl until the slices are evenly coated in the sugar mix. Transfer the slices to the sheet pan, ensuring they cover the pan evenly.

In a large bowl, combine the brown sugar, pecans, flour, oats, cornstarch and salt. Add the butter and maple syrup. Use your hands to combine and break up the butter. The mixture should turn into large crumbs.

When the mixture is crumb-like, scatter it over the sliced apples and push the batter into the apples slightly. Place the sheet pan into the oven to bake for 30 to 35 minutes, until the apples are soft and the topping is golden. Serve with custard or ice cream.

Cream Cheese Brownies

This is a recipe that I know won't disappoint. Pairing chocolate with cream cheese is glorious. The texture is heavenly and having chopped dates throughout provides some gooeyness. Don't worry if you don't get perfect swirls. These brownies will still taste delicious however they end up looking.

Yield: 12 brownies

Dairy-free butter, for greasing

2 cups (250 g) all-purpose flour

1½ tsp (7 g) baking powder

¾ cup (65 g) cacao powder

½ cup + 1 tbsp (125 g) light brown sugar

Pinch of salt

2 cups (480 ml) dairy-free milk

1¼ cups (210 g) dark chocolate chips/chunks, melted

½ cup (75 g) chopped dates

¾ cup (175 g) dairy-free cream cheese

2 tbsp (30 ml) maple syrup

1 tsp vanilla extract

1 tbsp (10 g) confectioners' sugar

Dairy-free ice cream

Preheat the oven to 350°F (180°C or gas mark 4) and grease a half sheet pan (13 x 18 inch [33 x 45 cm]) with dairy-free butter or line with parchment paper.

In a large bowl, combine the flour, baking powder, cacao powder, brown sugar and salt. Add the milk and stir to combine, then add the melted chocolate and chopped dates. Stir to combine, then put to one side.

In a medium bowl, combine the cream cheese, maple syrup, vanilla and confectioners' sugar.

Pour the chocolate brownie mixture into the sheet pan and spread the batter evenly into all four corners. Drizzle the cream cheese mixture in lines from one short side of the pan to the other. Drizzle approximately eight lines, then using a bread knife draw lines in the opposite direction through the cream cheese lines to create swirls.

Place the pan in the oven to bake for 15 minutes, or until firm but still a bit gooey inside. Allow the brownies to cool for 5 minutes before carefully slicing and serving with dairy-free ice cream.

Berry Crumble Slabs

This is one of those recipes that is good for the soul. With a slight sourness coming through from the berries, paired against a sweet crispy crumble topping, this recipe will make you smile. I used both walnuts and pecans but feel free to double up on one or the other if that's easier. Here in the UK, this is an example of a dessert that would be served after our Sunday dinner, mainly because it's easy and quick to make, yet still has that yummy "wow" factor.

Yield: 12 servings

¾ cup + 1 tbsp (185 g) dairy-free butter, plus more for greasing

2½ cups (310 g) all-purpose flour

1½ cups (335 g) superfine sugar, divided

½ tsp salt

1½ tsp (4 g) ground cinnamon

¾ cup (70 g) ground almonds/almond meal

4½ cups (650 g) frozen blueberries and/or blackberries

4 tbsp (40 g) cornstarch

1 tbsp (15 ml) vanilla extract

Juice from 1 lemon

½ cup (60 g) chopped walnuts

½ cup (55 g) chopped pecans

Dairy-free ice cream

Preheat the oven to 350°F (180°C or gas mark 4) and grease a half sheet pan (13 x 18 inch [33 x 45 cm]) with dairy-free butter or line with parchment paper.

In a large bowl, combine the flour, 1 cup (225 g) of the sugar, salt, ground cinnamon and ground almonds. Transfer to a blender or food processor and add the butter. Pulse until a crumb-like mixture forms and there are no lumps of butter.

Transfer two-thirds of the mixture to the sheet pan and flatten, ensuring the whole base of the pan is evenly covered.

In a medium bowl, combine the frozen berries, cornstarch, vanilla and lemon juice. When combined, scatter the berries over the base in the sheet pan.

Add the chopped walnuts and pecans to the reserved one-third of the base mix. Then scatter it over the top of the berries. Place the pan in the oven to bake for 20 minutes or until the berries have blistered and the top is golden. Allow the crumble to cool for 10 to 15 minutes before slicing and serving with ice cream.

Apple Galette with Salted Caramel

This warm apple cinnamon-y dessert is perfection! While you can use store-bought caramel, I've also included optional directions to make your own with a second pan. If you choose to make your own caramel sauce, this rich salted caramel has the most gorgeous texture thanks to the coconut milk (make sure it's full fat). The chopped hazelnuts add an element of crunch but feel free to use any chopped nuts if hazelnuts aren't your thing.

Yield: 6 servings

Pastry

1½ cups (200 g) all-purpose flour, plus more for rolling

⅓ cup (40 g) confectioners' sugar

½ tsp salt

½ cup (100 g) dairy-free butter, chilled

2 tbsp (30 ml) ice-cold water

1 tbsp (15 ml) extra virgin olive oil

Salted Caramel

1 cup (220 g) light brown sugar

1⅓ cups (330 ml) full-fat canned coconut milk

½ tsp salt

Filling

2 medium apples (Gala or Honeycrisp)

Juice from 1 lemon

1 tsp ground cinnamon

¼ cup (55 g) light brown sugar

¼ cup (30 g) chopped hazelnuts

In a large bowl, combine the flour, confectioners' sugar and salt. Add the butter and, using your hands, combine the ingredients until crumbs form.

Add the cold water 1 tablespoon (15 ml) at a time until the crumbs begin to clump together. Add the olive oil and form the dough into a ball. Cover and place the dough into the refrigerator for 1 hour to chill.

If making, prepare the caramel. In a large saucepan over a high heat mix the sugar and coconut milk. Bring to the boil and then turn the heat down to medium. Leave to simmer and caramelize for 15 minutes, stirring every 5 minutes. Add the salt, combine and take off the heat to cool.

Core and slice the apples, and place in a large bowl with the lemon juice, ground cinnamon and light brown sugar and toss them to coat.

When the dough has chilled for about 45 minutes, preheat the oven to 350°F (180°C or gas mark 4). Line a sheet pan with parchment paper.

Sprinkle some flour onto a work surface and, using a rolling pin, roll the chilled dough mixture out to the size of a dinner plate. Place a dinner plate on top of the pastry and cut around it to get a perfectly round shape. Transfer the pastry carefully onto the parchment-lined sheet pan.

Arrange the apple slices in the center of the pastry, leaving a 1-inch (2.5-cm) gap around the edge. Fold the pastry edges in over the apples and pinch as you go until all the edges are folded inward.

Place the sheet pan in the oven to bake for 25 minutes. When it is done, drizzle with the salted caramel and chopped hazelnuts.

Acknowledgments

My biggest thank you goes to those who have taken their time to make my recipes and spread the word about them. Your support means the world to me, and I've made some friendships and relationships that I'll cherish forever along the way. I wouldn't have been given the opportunity to write this cookbook if not for my online cheerleaders and loyal followers.

To my soon-to-be-husband, Tom: Who would have thought that our first ever date all those years back ended by eating chicken nuggets on a bench outside the station? How our lives have changed! Thank you for supporting every decision I make, and for making me the happiest girl alive. I wouldn't be where I am today without you.

I need to give a huge thank you to my amazing mum, Gill, for telling me to follow my dreams and quit my job that time we were on a girly holiday in 2019. You've brought up two crazily ambitious children, and we are forever grateful for the work ethic you instilled in us.

To my late Nan, Dorothy, for sharing my passion for baking (and eating!). I miss telling you all the new things I've made and catching up on our favorite cooking and baking shows. Thank you for teaching me that there is always room for dessert. I hope I'm doing you and Grandad proud.

Thank you to my wonderful in-laws, Patrick and Linda, for embracing my dietary requirements with open arms. I'm not sure you knew what vegan was before me, but you have championed every step of my journey with so much encouragement, and I am so grateful for your generosity.

And last, to Page Street Publishing, thank you for believing that I could bring this book to life with the enormous help of your team. You guys will forever hold a special space in my heart.

About the Author

Lucy, or Luce as she is most commonly known, is a plant-based recipe developer and food photographer. She strives to create tasty recipes and to teach people that eating plant-based doesn't need to be bland or repetitive. Lucy is an Essex girl at heart, who now lives in the northeast of England with her partner, Tom, and two dogs. If she's not in the kitchen creating recipes, she can be found exploring and enjoying the beautiful local surroundings. You can follow her on social media @whatluceeats or check out her blog www.whatluceeats.com to find more of her recipes.

Index